SAC'S FIGHTER PLANES AND THEIR OPERATIONS

BY

ROBERT J. BOYD

OFFICE OF THE HISTORIAN
HEADQUARTERS STRATEGIC AIR COMMAND
1 AUGUST 1988

TABLE OF CONTENTS

ILLUSTRATIONS

APPENDIXIES

INTRODUCTION

The Strategic Air Command (SAC) is best known to the public for its bombers and missiles. Slightly less well known are its air refueling tankers and reconnaissance aircraft. Least known are the strategic fighters which served the command both as escort fighters for the bombers and later as weapon delivery aircraft, and finally in a base defense role.

SAC's early war plans proposed to operate the bombers from advanced staging bases in Europe, Africa, and Asia. To test the plans and those bases, the bombers regularly deployed to them in rotation exercises. The fighters also deployed to advanced bases for exercises in the escort mission, then later in exercises for their nuclear weapons role as well.

Throughout the 13 years that fighters were in SAC, there was one major problem. the fighters assigned to SAC were modern but still inadequate to meet established SAC standards and requirements. It was not until the arrival of the F-101 that SAC acquired a fighter aircraft that had the potential to meet requirements. The F-101 came on the scene in May 1957, and in July of that year, SAC abandoned the fighters. Technological advances in bomber aircraft and changes in tactics had eliminated the need for strategic fighters. However, fighters reappeared under SAC aegis again in 1958 when the 497th Squadron at Torrejon and the 431st Squadron at Zaragoza were assigned. Based at these Spanish bases, both were there for the purpose of base defense.

The Strategic Air Command was established on 21 March 1946. For the next 11 years, until 1 July 1957, fighter groups and wings were assigned as part of the SAC force. In those years, 17 separate fighter units were assigned. Twelve of the 17 were regular organizations, four were Air National Guard (ANG) fighter wings that were called to active federal service during the Korean War, and one was a U. S. Air Force Reserve (USAFR) Corollary Group. The number assigned to SAC at any one time varied, depending upon authorizations, but the peak strength was seven fighter wings assigned at one time which occurred both in 1951 and again in 1955-1956.

Organizationally, SAC's fighter program went through four major periods. The first was from 1946 to 1950 and was characterized by a lack of stability. The second was from 1950 to 1953 and the dominant theme was the Korean War and the USAF expansion. The third period covered from the end of the Korean War to 1957. The final period was from 1958 to 1960 when two squadrons were assigned for the defense of two Spanish bases, Torrejon and Zaragoza.

2

SAC Fighter Program

The postwar period was one of reorganization to adjust the military forces to peacetime. The structure of the SAC fighter program within USAAF and USAF was determined by the authorizations and funding provided by Congress. In the first four years after the war, congressional authorizations for the number of combat and troop carrier groups rose and fell.

USAAF and USAF Group/Wing Programs[*]

Congressional authorizations for FY 1946 allowed for a total of 54 groups, and this was increased to 63 for the next fiscal year. In the following year, FY 1948, authorizations peaked at 70 wings, the highest authorized in this first four-year period. For FY 1949, Congress reduced authorizations to 56 wings and reduced it again in the following year to 48. Authorization however, was not matched by funding which seldom provided enough to maintain full complements. For example, the FY 1950 authorizations allowed 48 wings, but funds were sufficient for only 42 combat-effective wings.

Within the congressional authorizations were those for the bomber and fighter units in SAC. The War Department established SAC in March 1946, but until November there was normal postwar confusion about SAC unit authorizations as demobilization took its toll. Meanwhile, Headquarters SAC made ambitious plans for the organization of 21 very heavy bombardment groups, three very long-range reconnaissance groups, and 12 very long-range fighter groups. This plan was for internal SAC use only and in July 1946 Headquarters SAC sent a refined proposal to USAAF. This was a long-range projection and it reduced fighter groups from 12 to nine. A response from USAAF was delayed until late fall and officially on 25 November 1946, the USAAF plan made a drastic reduction to three fighter groups. This gave SAC a base on which to build, but the delays, reductions, and instability set the tone for the first four years.

---

[*] On 15 August 1947, SAC fighter units were reorganized on the Hobson Plan, wing headquarters with the same numerical designator as the tactical groups were organized and placed in a supervisory capacity over all combat and support elements on a base. The combat groups were made subordinate to the wings. The group organizations were inactivated on 16 June 1952.

Congressional authorizations had changed, but the changes in the fighter strengths did not parallel them. In relation to the total group/wing authorizations, SAC's were as follows:

Fiscal Year	USAAF/USAF* Authorizations	SAC Fighter Group Wing Authorizations
1946	54	3
1947	63	5
1948	70	2
1949	56	2
1950	48	2

As a consequence of these shifts, fighter wings assigned to the command in the four-year period were as follows:

Fighter Units	Initial Base** Assignment	Dates Assigned to SAC
1946		
56th	Selfridge	1 Mar 46 – 1 Dec 48
82nd	Bolling	27 Jun 46 – 22 Aug 49
4th	Andrews	9 Sep 46 – 1 Dec 48
1947		
27th	Andrews	25 Jun 47 – 1 Jul 57
33rd	Andrews	25 Aug 47 – 1 Dec 48
1949		
1st	March	1 Mar 49 – 1 Jul 50

SAC's decline in authorizations from five fighter wings to two in 1948 was a direct result of the USAF requirement to build up the Continental Air Command (CONAC) for the air defense mission. SAC's authorizations for fighter wings remained at two until well into the Korean War.

---

* The United States Air Force (USAF) came into being 18 September, 1947.

** Effective 13 January 1948, all installations designated Army Air Fields (AAF) and Army Air Bases (AAB) were redesignated Air Force Bases (AFB), DAF GO 2, 13 Jan 48.

4

Policies and Requirements

In 1946, the first-line fighters were the P-47N and the P-51H. These aircraft had proven themselves during World War II by successfully conducting bomber escort missions for the B-17 and B-24 bombers in the European theater and by limited escort of B-29s in the Pacific Ocean areas. Technology had passed by them and the P-47 and P-51 were no longer adequate for escort missions. First, the 1946 SAC bomber force consisted of B-29s whose speed, altitude, and range were such that the first-line fighters were only marginal in performance of escort duties. Programs were underway to update the bomber force with the B-50 and B-36 which would restrict the fighter abilities even further. Besides, the bombers would soon be the jet-propelled aircraft of the B-40 series which would limit the World War II fighters even more. Second, the advent of jet propulsion in the German ME-262, placed the propellor-driven aircraft in an obsolescent status. Germany was not alone in the development of jet engines, and the use of the operational fighters in the closing stages of World War II led to the logical assumption that an enemy force in the future would have jet propelled interceptors in operation. In recognition of jet superiority, the Army Air Forces noted, in mid-1946, that the first-line fighters were scheduled for retirement by 1948. As a consequence, no further procurement was planned. Headquarters USAAF predicted that the first-line fighters by the end of fiscal year 1949 would be first-generation jets, the P-80, P-84, and P-86.

The crux of the matter was that all these fighters, jet and conventional, were products of World War II technology. None could provide continuous close escort for bombers with conventional engines because of speed differences. Limited range of operations also meant that the jet fighters could not cover bombers beyond a radius of 700 to 900 miles. Under these conditions, one acceptable solution was to limit bomber operations within the limited radius of action of fighters during daylight missions. For those missions beyond fighter range, night bomber operations were recommended on a temporary basis. Headquarters SAC concurred but recommended that SAC's fighter units be modernized with jet aircraft as soon as possible because the current equipment was not adequate for defense against jet-propelled enemy fighters. Even though inadequate, SAC fighter units would continue to use what was possessed, but research to modernize the fighters was needed.

Protection of the bomber force from modern jet interceptors was a serious problem. Design and development of a satisfactory long-range jet fighter escort represented a solution, but the task would take time, money, and advanced technology. Regardless, Headquarters SAC, in 1949, stated a requirement for the development of such a fighter.

SAC's requirements included modern features, but the radius of action was specified at 1500 nautical miles without refueling even though refueling was to be incorporated. Aside from these, the requirement stressed that the armament installation ". . . be designed solely to fit the intended tactical use to which penetration fighters are to be committed by this command." The requirement reemphasized this by concluding:

Versatility considerations aimed toward making this airplane more effective in other tactical situations should not be permitted to influence the choice of armament for those airplanes consigned to this command.

In early 1950, three prototypes (McDonnell's F-88, Lockheed's F-90, and North American's F-93) were test flown to determine which of the three was most satisfactory as a penetration fighter. The pilots, who represented several commands, concluded that the F-88 was most suitable for the penetration mission. Even though the Air Materiel Command fighter evaluation meeting in July 1950 concurred with the pilot's conclusions, Headquarters USAF and the Board of Senior Officers determined in September 1950 that the aircraft could not perform the mission and, therefore, they would not permit procurement. Instead, F-84Gs, which were refuelable, were to be assigned to SAC. Long-range planning indicated that the faster F-84F would eventually replace them.

Shortly thereafter, the Korean War introduced some changes. The experience of fighters against the MIG-15 confirmed the judgment of Headquarters SAC that none of the fighters in the USAF procurement program had been designed with the necessary speed and range for the escort mission. Thus, none would meet the performance desired for strategic escort.

As a direct result of the information obtained from experiences in Korea, a conference was held in the Pentagon in February 1951 to discuss escort fighters. The conclusions were the strongest recommendations to that time for an adequate escort fighter. They were:

1. The present and projected integral Bomber Defense System cannot effectively cope with coordinated fighter attacks.

2. Strategic Air Command's bomber forces, in carrying out assigned missions, will suffer an unacceptable loss rate during daylight conditions over enemy territory defended by interceptors.

3. An effective fighter escort to augment the integral Bomber Defense System must be provided.

4. Neither current escort fighters or programmed escort fighters have a capability of adequately defending bombers during this time period.

6

5. An urgent requirement exists for an improved escort fighter capable of providing adequate bobmber defense.

After a delay, Headquarters USAF approved the development of the F-88 (renamed F-101A) during FY 1952. On its first flight, 29 September 1954, it attained supersonic speed. Headquarters USAF had allotted sufficient F-101A aircraft to SAC to equip two fighter wings. The 27th Strategic Fighter Wing (SFW) would be converted first. The first airplanes were to arrive in October 1956 but repeated delays stalled the delivery until May 1957. When delivered, the first F-101A was immediately "loaned" to the Air Training Command. Three more F-101As were assigned to the 27th SFW in June 1957. On 1 July 1957, the 27th, along with other fighter wings, was relieved from assignment to SAC and assigned to TAC.

During the years that fighters were assigned to SAC, none of those assigned were fully capable of adequate escort. Shortly after the F-101A, which had the greatest potential for the escort mission, became operational and was assigned to the command, the fighter mission terminated.

SAC's Fighter Organizations, 1946-1950

The first fighter unit assigned to SAC was the 56th Fighter Group commanding the 61st, 62nd, and 63rd Fighter Squadrons, Single Engine. This World War II organization had been returned to the United States from Europe and inactivated on 18 October 1945 as part of the demobilization. When it was assigned to SAC and the Fifteenth Air Force and activated on 1 May 1946, it was authorized 75 P-51 aircraft as unit equipment (UE).* As a matter of fact, it was not equipped at that time. The commander of the group, Colonel David C. Schilling, stated in 1956 that when the group began, ". . . in 1946, our 56th Fighter Group-- the command's only fighter wing--was equipped with 21 worn-out P-47s and ten borrowed P-51s." These were leftover World War II propellor-driven aircraft. Furthermore, none of these first 31 fighter planes were officially assigned to the 56th Fighter Group. The officially assigned P-51H airplanes did not begin to arrive at Selfridge Army Field until June 1946, and the group did not attain its full UE authorization of 75 aircraft until the last days of September 1946. By the end of

---

* Unit Equipment or UE indicates the number of operating active aircraft authorized to a unit for performance of its mission. SAC's fighter squadrons were standard throughout the history of fighters in the command. Each squadron possessed a UE of 25 aircraft and each group/wing commanded three squadrons.

the year, there were 82 P-51Hs assigned to the 56th Fighter Group. These 82 fighters represented the tactical fighter plane assets of SAC on 31 December 1946, because the other two groups assigned to the command possessed no aircraft.

The second fighter group assigned to SAC was the 82nd Fighter Group which commanded the 95th, 96th, and 97th Fighter Squadrons, Two Engine. The 82nd Fighter Group had been a World War II P-38 organization which had been inactivated in Italy on 9 September 1945. It was assigned to SAC and Bolling Field in an inactive status on 27 June 1946. On 21 October 1946, it was reassigned from Bolling to Andrews Field, but it remained in an inactive status all through 1946.

The third fighter unit assigned to SAC was the 4th Fighter Group which commanded the 334th, 335th, and 336th Fighter Squadrons, Single Engine. This group had served in Europe in World War II and had been equipped with P-51s. It was returned to the United States and inactivated on 10 November 1945 as part of the general demobilization. It was assigned to SAC and activated at Selfridge AAF on 9 September 1946. It was first scheduled to be equipped with the modern P-47N, but later that month the UE changed from P-47N to P-51H. Meanwhile, the 4th had started building up until by the end of November, 80 personnel were assigned. A policy change in November stopped the progress because the 4th was not to be equipped with propellor-driven aircraft in the postwar period. Instead, it was to be equipped with the P-80A, the first operational production jet aircraft of the U.S. forces. As a consequence of this change, the buildup of the 4th Fighter Group was reversed and the group was reduced in December 1946 to minimum manning with one officer and one airman.

SAC thus ended 1946 with three fighter groups assigned. Two of them were further assigned to the Fifteenth Air Force and one was assigned directly to Headquarters SAC. Of these three, only one possessed aircraft. As a matter of fact, one of its squadrons--the 62nd Fighter Squadron, Single Engine--was deployed to Alaska on six months temporary duty to conduct testing and training operations in conjunction with the 28th Bombardment Group, Very Heavy. On 31 December 1946, there were 82 P-51H aircraft assigned to that one fighter group, which included the 27 in Alaska. These constituted the official initial fighter force in SAC, but vast organizational changes were under way for 1947.

The first organizational change in 1947 took place on 1 April, when the 4th Fighter Group was relieved from assignment to the Fifteenth Air Force, assigned to Headquarters SAC, and moved from Selfridge AAF to Andrews Field. Three weeks later on 23 April 1947, the group's three fighter squadrons were redesignated from "Single Engine" to "Jet-Propelled," making it the first jet-propelled unit in SAC. The unit equipment was changed from a 75 UE P-51H organization to a 75 UE P-80A unit. This was only a paper conversion since no aircraft had been assigned to it in the postwar era. On 24 April 1947, the 56th Fighter Group's three squadrons were also redesignated in the same manner. But for the 56th the change from P-51s to P-80s was a conversion program of enough importance to call the 62nd Fighter Squadron back to Selfridge AAF from its temporary duty station at Ladd Field and Mile 26 in Alaska before its full tour was completed.

Since the 82nd Fighter Group was assigned to SAC at Andrews, though in an inactive status, the move of the 4th Fighter Group to Andrews would have placed two fighter groups on that base. Consequently, on 12 April 1947, the 82nd Fighter Group was moved to Grenier Field, New Hampshire, removed from inactive status, assigned to the Fifteenth Air Force, and the Commanding General of the Fifteenth was directed to activate and organize the 82nd Fighter Group.

On 1 August 1947, the 82nd was relieved from assignment to the Fifteenth Air Force and assigned to the 94th Combat Bombardment Wing, Provisional, with no change in station. Two weeks later on 15 August almost everything connected with the 82nd was changed. First, the 82nd Fighter Wing was assigned to SAC, designated and organized. Second, the 82nd Fighter Group and the three fighter squadrons were assigned to the 82nd Wing. Third, the 82nd Fighter Wing was reorganized and redesignated from "Two Engine" to "Single Engine" and the UE was changed to 75 UE P-51H fighter aircraft. Also on 15 August 1947, the 94th Combat Bombardment Wing, Provisional, was inactivated. As a consequence, the 82nd Fighter Wing was assigned directly to SAC. The first P-51H aircraft began arriving at Grenier Field in September 1947, and by the end of the year the full UE was in place.

Two new organizations were assigned to SAC in 1947. One was the 27th Fighter Group and the other was the 33rd Fighter Group. The 27th was a World War II P-51 fighter organization which had been assigned to United States Air Forces in Europe (USAFE) in the postwar period. In June 1947, it was returned to the U.S. without personnel and equipment and assigned to SAC at Andrews with the 522nd, 523rd, and 524th Fighter Squadrons, Single Engine. On 16 July 1947, the group was relieved from its original assignment to Headquarters SAC, assigned to the Eighth Air Force, and moved to Kearney AAF, Nebraska, without personnel or equipment. The 27th Fighter Wing was designated, organized, and assigned to SAC and the 27th Fighter Group was assigned to the wing. Concurrently, the unit was redesignated "Two Engine" from "Single Engine." In this instance, the 27th's UE was 75 P-82 fighters rather than the P-51s from previous organization. Equipping was slow and by the end of 1947 only one of the P-82s, the "Double Mustang," was possessed by SAC.

The second newly-assigned fighter unit was the 33rd Fighter Group which raised the total fighter units assigned to SAC to five. It, too, had been assigned to USAFE but was transferred and assigned to SAC at Andrews Field on 25 August without personnel or equipment. It was further assigned to the Eighth Air Force and stationed at Roswell AAF, effective 16 September 1947. On 15 October 1947, the 33rd Fighter Wing was designated and assigned to SAC. It was further assigned to the Eighth Air Force and organized at Roswell AAF on 5 November. The 33rd Fighter Group and the 58th, 59th, and 60th Fighter Squadrons, Single Engine, were assigned and reorganized two days later on 7 November. This P-51 organization possessed a standard UE of 75 fighter aircraft, and it was fully equipped with fighters at the end of the year. On 17 November 1947, it was attached to the 509th Bombardment Wing, Very Heavy.

The second year of SAC had been a bustling one so far as the organization of the fighter strength was concerned. At the end of the year, SAC commanded five fighter wings, five groups, and 15 squadrons. Four wings and 12 squadrons were fully equipped with aircraft. By 31 December 1947, SAC's fighter aircraft assets totaled 230 P-51Hs, 120 P-80As, and one P-82E.

The rapid buildup of the SAC fighter force by the end of 1947 was reversed the following year. On 1 December 1948, three of the five fighter wings were relieved from assignment to SAC and assigned to the Continental Air Command (CONAC) for air defense purposes. The three units were the 4th, 33rd, and 56th. On 1 August 1948, the 33rd Fighter Wing was redesignated from "Single Engine" to "Jet." The wing was equipped with F-84Bs, the first in SAC. Then, on 16 November 1948, the wing moved from Roswell AFB to Otis AFB, Massachusetts. Two weeks later it was assigned to CONAC.

The 4th and 56th Fighter Wings were the two P-80 aircraft units in SAC and were transferred out because of the inadequacies of that airplane (see below). This year also saw the end of the activity of Headquarters SAC as an agency of direct unit command for the fighter units. At the end of 1948, SAC possessed substantially fewer aircraft than the previous year. There were 81 P-82Es, 52 P-51Hs, seven F-84s, and one P-80.

Three significant organizational changes pertaining to the figher force occurred in 1949. On 1 May, Headquarters USAF assigned March AFB to SAC. Stationed at that base was the 1st Fighter Wing, with the 1st Fighter Group, and the 27th, 71st, and 94th Fighter Squadrons. Two of these squadrons traced lineage back to World War I. Concurrent with the assignment of the base, the 1st Fighter Wing was also assigned to SAC. It was equipped with a UE of 75 F-86 interceptors. This unit was not considered part of the SAC escort fleet. The range of the F-86 was severely limited, and when not grounded it was an excellent interceptor aircraft. Further evidence of its fundamental nature was the fact that, on 16 April 1950, the wing was redesignated the 1st Fighter-Interceptor Wing.

The second major organizational change in 1949 was the transfer of the 82nd Fighter Wing. On 22 August it was relieved from assignment to SAC and assigned to CONAC with no change in station from Grenier AFB.

A third major change was the activation and assignment of a USAF Reserve Corollary Unit. On 27 June 1949, the 87th Fighter Group with the 535th Fighter Squadron and the 524th Fighter Squadron, Two Engine, at Bergstrom AFB. This was the only USAF Reserve Corollary fighter unit assigned to SAC. It had been a World War II pilot replacement training unit and was disbanded in 1944. It was reconstituted on 16 May 1949, and allotted to the reserve. It was activated as a reserve unit on the date it was assigned to SAC.

One internal organizational change occurred in 1949. In December, the 522nd, 523rd, and 524th Fighter Squadrons of the 27th Fighter Wing were redesignated from "Two Engine" to "Jet" and the UE changed from F-82 to F-84. Officially, this redesignation ended the era of the propellor-driven fighter of the regular USAF organizations in SAC. With a short interruption during the Korean War, SAC's fighter organizations would remain completely equipped with jet-propelled aircraft. Conversion of the 27th Fighter Wing, however, was a complicated process. At the end of 1949, SAC commanded two fighter wings and one USAFR Corollary Unit. One fighter wing was equipped with F-86 interceptors. The other was in the process of converting to the F-84. The total number of fighters assigned to the command on 31 December 1949 was 152.

Before SAC's fighters were applied to the Korean War, there were some organizational changes. On 16 March 1950, the 87th Fighter Group and the 535th Fighter Squadron, Two Engine, were redesignated "Jet" and the UE was changed to F-84s. In May and June, both the group and squadron were designated a "fully organized USAFR Corollary Unit." On 1 July 1950, the 1st Fighter-Interceptor Wing was relieved from assignment to SAC and assigned to Continental Air Command for air defense. Further evidence of the mission capabilities of the F-86 was that, on 1 February 1950, the 27th Fighter Wing and all subordinate units were redesignated "Fighter-Escort" on 16 April 1950. With the loss of the 1st Fighter-Interceptor Wing, Headquarters USAF assigned a replacement to SAC, the 31st Fighter-Bomber Wing, 31st Fighter-Bomber Group, and the 307th, 308th, and 309th Fighter-Bomber Squadrons. They were relieved from assignment to Continental Air Command, assigned to SAC, further assigned to the Second Air Force (first fighter unit assigned to the Second Air Force), and stationed at Turner AFB. On 16 July 1950, all units of the 31st were redesignated "Fighter-Escort." This was a fully-equipped organization and possessed a UE of 75 F-84 aircraft.

On 25 June 1950, the North Korean forces attacked South Korea. This event signaled the end of the first period of the SAC fighters and their reorganizations. In these four years, the existence of the SAC fighter program followed an erratic course with six separate fighter wings and five different types of aircraft being operated by the units. Furthermore, none of the fighter aircraft was ideally suited for SAC's escort duties with the B-29s, B-50s, and B-36s. By 1950, the instability that had characterized the first four years virtually disappeared and a more stable program replaced it. Rather than have the fighter units scattered on individual bases, Turner and Bergstrom AFBs were firmly established as SAC's main fighter bases, with one wing based on each. However, they were prepared for expansion and those two bases would support the bulk of SAC fighters for most of the next seven years that fighters would remain in the command. Besides, the Korean War triggered a USAF expansion program in late 1950 that was increased again in 1952 and again in 1954. Each of the increases affected SAC's fighter wing program.

SAC's Fighter Organizations and the Korean War, 1950-1953

When the Korean War broke out in late June 1950, the demand for combat ready organizations included bombers and fighters as well as ground forces. The B-29 bomber units deployed almost immediately and, in November 1950, the first of many of the SAC fighter wings went over. These demands, as well as the seriousness of the situation, served as partial cause for increases in the SAC fighter wing authorizations. Furthermore, the USAF wing program expanded in this period to encompass 95 wings, which included seven fighter wings for SAC. These were added in the following manner.

In October 1950, the 27th Fighter Escort Wing was alerted for transfer to Japan and Korea and was committed to augment the Far East Air Forces (FEAF) fighters there as a replacement. The 12th Fighter-Escort Wing, 12th Fighter-Escort Group, 559th 560th, and 561st Fighter-Escort Squadrons were assigned to SAC, the Second Air Force, and activated at Turner AFB. The 12th was activated as a 75 UE F-84E aircraft unit. This organization was originally constituted as the 12th Bombardment Group, Light, during World War II. It had been inactivated on 22 January 1946 and activated again on 19 May 1947. In the last activation, it was not manned and was later inactivated on 10 September 1948. After its activation and assignment to SAC, it did not remain at Turner AFB long. On 5 December 1950, the 12th moved from Turner to Bergstrom AFB. Even though the 27th Fighter-Escort Wing was detailed to Korea and FEAF, this gave the SAC fighter force three wings. In March and April 1951, four Air National Guard fighter wings were relieved from assignment to Continental Air Command and assigned to SAC.

The first of these was the 131st Fighter Wing, with the 131st Fighter Group, and the 110th, 170th, and 192nd Fighter Squadrons. This unit was assigned to SAC, the Eighth Air Force, on 10 March 1951. It was stationed at Bergstrom and equipped with a UE Of 75 F-51D aircraft. A month later, 9 April, the components of this unit were redesignated "Fighter-Bomber." On 4 August the 131st Fighter-Bomber Wing was transferred from the Eighth Air Force to the Fifteenth Air Force and moved from Bergstrom AFB to George AFB, California.

The second Air National Guard (ANG) unit assigned to SAC, on 16 March 1951, was the 108th Fighter Wing, with the 108th Fighter Group, and the 141st 149th, and 153rd Fighter Squadrons, Single Engine. This 75 UE F-47D organization was also relieved from assignment to the Continental Air Command and assigned to SAC, the Eighth Air Force, and the 40th Air Division at Turner AFB, Georgia. Paralleling the 131st, the 108th, too, was redesignated a "Fighter-Bomber" organization on 16 May 1951.

The third ANG organization was the 132nd Fighter Wing, with the 132nd Fighter Group, and the 124th, 173rd, and 174th Fighter Squadrons. It was relieved from assignment to the Continental Air Command, assigned to SAC, the Eighth Air Force, on 16 April 1952, and stationed at Dow AFB, Maine. The UE of the 132nd Fighter Wing was unusual. Two of the fighter squadrons, the 124th and 173rd, were equipped with F-51D aircraft and were designated "Single Engine." The other squadron, the 174th, was equipped with F-84B/C and was designated "Jet." This was the only such organization in SAC. In the same manner as the other Air National Guard units assigned to the command, the 132nd Fighter Wing and its subordinate units were redesignated "Fighter-Bomber" on 1 June 1951.

The last ANG organization assigned to SAC was the 146th Fighter Wing, with the 146th Fighter Group, and the 178th, 186th, and 190th Fighter Squadrons, Single Engine. This 75 UE F-51D unit was relieved from assignment to the Continental Air Command and assigned to SAC, the Second Air Force, 40th Air Division, on 17 April 1951, and stationed at Moody AFB, Georgia. It was redesignated "Fighter-Bomber" on 1 June 1951.

Of the 12 ANG fighter squadrons assigned to SAC, all but one were equipped with piston-engined aircraft. This retrogression was expected to be only temporary and conversion to jet fighters was expected to be accomplished as soon as possible, probably not later than 1952. Before any conversion could occur, Headquarters USAF informed SAC that Tactical Air Command (TAC) needed four wings of fighters to support Army ground training. The four ANG fighter wings were the obvious choice and they were selected. Thus, several months after acquiring four units, they were relieved from assignment to SAC and assigned to the Tactical Air Command reducing SAC's fighter wings to three. Effective dates of the transfer were 15 and 16 November 1951.

The addition of the four Air National Guard units to SAC's fighter force produced an unusual arrangement of aircraft assets for 30 June 1951. On that date, there were 170 F-84s assigned to SAC which did not include the F-84s in Korea, but it did include the 16 F-84B/C aircraft of the 174th Fighter Squadron, Jet, of the 132nd Fighter Wing. The other eleven squadrons of the four ANG wings were equipped with 80 F-47Ds and 107 F-51D aircraft. The conventional aircraft were transferred out of the command when the units were transferred to the Tactical Air Command. From that time forward to the demise of fighters in SAC, the mainstay of the SAC fighter force was the F-84.

For a short period in 1951, from the time of assignment of the fourth ANG wing until the four units were transferred out, the Strategic Air Command had attained its authorized level of seven fighter wings under the USAF 95-wing expansion program.

An additional change in internal organization occurred in 1951. On 1 May, the 87th Fighter-Escort Group and the 535th Fighter-Escort Squadron were ordered into active federal military service for 21 months, assigned to SAC and the Eighth Air Force. On 25 June 1951, they were inactivated at Bergstrom AFB and the personnel absorbed by other Eighth Air Force units.

One internal organizational change occurred in 1952. On 16 June, all combat groups in the bomber and fighter combat wings were inactivated. The squadrons were made directly responsible to the wing commanders and headquarters without the intermediate group headquarters. Also in 1952, preparations were made to increase the forces starting in FY 1953.

Organizational problems were associated with the enormous expansion of the number of SAC's units during the Korean War. Deployments during the conflict had provided additional evidence that changes in the existing organizational structure were imperative to maintain maximum effectiveness. As a solution for those bases with two combat wings assigned, Headquarters SAC in early 1951 established small air division headquarters on those bases. These air divisions served as an intermediate echelon of command, as a connecting link between the combat wings and the numbered air force headquarters. The air divisions were designed to supervise, direct, and coordinate the operations of the assigned combat wings and an air base group, and the fixed medical facility were directly under the air division commander.[85] In the period of the fighters in SAC, there were only two fighter air divisions, the 40th and the 42nd, located at Turner AFB and Bergstrom AFB, respectively.

Headquarters SAC activated the first fighter air division on 10 March 1951, more than a month after the activation of the first air divisions for the bombers. The first fighter air division was the 42nd, stationed at Bergstrom AFB, but no fighter wings were assigned to it unitl 9 April 1951. Then Headquarters SAC assigned the two fighter wings there to the division. The two were the regular USAF units, the 12th Fighter-Escort Wing, and the Air National Guard unit, the 131st Fighter-Bomber Wing. In the summer of 1951, the 27th Fighter-Escort Wing, formerly assigned to Bergstrom AFB, was in the process of returning from Korea and attachment to the Far East Forces, although without its aircraft. The prospect of three fighter wings on one base was one of overcrowding. To prevent that, Headquarters SAC transferred the 131st Fighter-Bomber Wing from the Eighth Air Force to the Fifteenth Air Force on 23 July 1951, and moved it from Bergstrom AFB to George AFB on 4 August 1951. Two days later on 6 August 1951, Headquarters SAC assigned the 27th Fighter-Escort Wing to the 42nd Air Division and stationed the wing at Bergstrom AFB. The 12th and the 27th wings thus assigned to the 42nd Air Division remained assigned to the division until 1 July 1957, when both wings were relieved from assignment to SAC and assigned to TAC. At the same time, the 42nd Air Division was inactivated.

The second fighter air division activated by SAC was the 40th Air Division, stationed at Turner AFB, effective 14 March 1951. On 16 March 1951, the 108th Fighter Wing was relieved from assignment to the Continental Air Command and assigned to SAC. Headquarters SAC further assigned this Air National Guard unit to the Second Air Force and the 40th Air Division. On 9 April 1951, Headquarters SAC also assigned the 31st Figher-Escort Wing to the air division, thereby giving it two fighter wings to command. When the 108th moved from Turner AFB, only the 31st remained assigned to the division, but the condition of a one-wing air division was only temporary. On 1 July 1952, Headquarters SAC activated the 508th Fighter-Escort Wing at Turner AFB, assigned it to the Second Air Force and the 40th Air Division. The 508th remained assigned to the air division until the wing was inactivated on 11 May 1956. On 1 April 1957, the 31st Strategic Fighter Wing was relieved from assignment to SAC and assigned to TAC. Concurrently, the 40th Air Division was inactivated.

The Last Years of SAC's Fighters, 1953-1957

The international and ideological inferences drawn from the Korean War led to a changed U.S. national policy and the military forces were increased, especially the Air Force. In June 1952, one of the more important changes came with the USAF expansion program leading to the ultimate goal of 143 combat wings. Under this expanded program, SAC was scheduled to activate three fighter wings and one fighter-reconnaissance wing during FY 1954 and to reach a peak strength of ten fighter wings during FY 1955. Before the buildup could develop beyond the initial stages, the Eisenhower administration took office in January 1953. It directed a reduction to an interim goal of 120 wings which was later increased to 137 wings. This economy measure resulted in the following changes in the SAC strategic fighter wing authorizations.

SAC Fighter Wing Program

	FY 53	FY 54	FY 55	FY 56
143-Wing Program	5	8	10	10
120/137-Wing Program	5	5	7	9

The actual number of wings in USAF at the end of each fiscal year as compared with the SAC fighter wings were as follows:

	FY 53	FY 54	FY 55	FY 56	FY 57
USAF Combat & Troop Carrier Wings	106	115	121	131	134
SAC Fighter Wings	5	6	7	6	0

At the end of FY 1952, there were three fighter-escort wings assigned to SAC: 12th, 27th, and 31st. In accordance with the USAF expansion program, SAC first activated the 508th Fighter-Escort Wing, with the 446th, 447th, and 448th Fighter-Escort Squadrons at Turner AFB on 1 July 1952 as an F-84 75 UE unit. It was assigned to the Second Air Force and the 40th Air Division. This increase in the number of active fighter wings to four was the beginning of the post-Korean War buildup.

In January 1953, a significant change in the primary mission of SAC's fighters produced a redesignation of the wings. The primary mission became the delivery of nuclear weapons in support of the strategic offensive. Escort of bombers became a secondary mission (see below for further discussion). On 20 January 1953, all fighter-escort units were redesignated strategic fighter wings and squadrons, indicative of the changed mission for the fighters as well as changed programs.

In building toward the goal of nine strategic fighter wings in FY 1956, SAC's initial step was to activate two wings in 1953, one in January and one in December. On 24 January 1953, SAC activated the 506th Strategic Fighter Wing, with the 457th, 458th, and 462nd Strategic Fighter Squadrons. It was assigned to SAC, Eighth Air Force, and stationed at Dow AFB, Maine. When activated in 1953, it was equipped with a 75 UE F-84 fleet.

The activation of these two wings in 1953 raised the SAC total of fighter wings to six, where it was to remain until the last fighter wing was activated in January 1955. There was one major difference with the 1955 activation. On 24 January 1955, SAC activated the 71st Strategic Reconnaissance Wing, Fighter, with the 25th and 82nd Strategic Reconnaissance Squadrons, Fighter, at Larson AFB, Washington. The UE for this organization was 25 RF-84F fighters for each squadron. The third squadron assigned was the 91st Strategic Reconnaissance Squadron, Fighter, which was one of the illustrious units in USAF. Its lineage was traced back to the 91st Aero Squadron which was organized on 21 August 1917. On 20 December 1954, the 91st Strategic Reconnaissance Squadron, Medium, Photographic, had been reassigned from FEAF to SAC, attached to the 407th Strategic Fighter Wing at Great Falls AFB, redesignated 91st Strategic Reconnaissance Squadron, Fighter, and reorganized. When the 71st Strategic Reconnaissance Wing, Fighter, was activated, the 91st Strategic Reconnaissance Squadron, Fighter, was assigned to it, even though the squadron did not move from Great Falls AFB to Larson AFB until mid-July 1955. The 91st was to become one of the most unusual squadrons in USAF. It was equipped with RBF-84K aircraft which were the fighters that were carried in the bomb bay of the B-36 in what came to be known as the Fighter Conveyor (FICON) project. Twenty-five RF-84F and 12 RB-36D aircraft were modified. The fighter was equipped with a retractable hook and the bomber was equipped with a trapeze. This combination permitted the fighter to be carried in the bomb bay of the bomber for a long distance closer to the target and, after the operational sortie, the bomber would recover the fighter and carry it to the home base. The fighters, first redesignated RBF-84F and later RF-84K, were assigned to the 91st Strategic Reconnaissance Squadron, Fighter. The bombers, first redesignated GRB-36D and later RB-36D, were assigned to the 348th Strategic Reconnaissance Squadron, Heavy, of the 99th Strategic Reconnaissance Wing, Heavy, stationed at Fairchild AFB.

Hookups between the two aircraft were problems. Because of the aircraft damage resulting from accidents during this part of the recovery operations, Headquarters SAC requested termination of this project. Headquarters USAF concurred in February 1956. The primary mission of the special units ended. The mission of the 71st Strategic Reconnaissance Wing, Fighter, was revised to eliminate the special operations.

On 1 March 1955, the 506th Strategic Fighter Wing and its three fighter squadrons moved from Dow AFB to Tinker AFB. The reason for this move was that the new F-84F aircraft required a longer runway for takeoff than the Dow facility could provide.

Air Refueling Squadrons, Strategic Fighter

The factor of adequate range for fighters employed as escorts for SAC's bombers proved to be as critical following World War II as it had during the war. SAC began air refueling for bombers in 1948 and the extension of range obtained by air refueling from a tanker aircraft had proved successful. Application of air refueling techniques to the jet fighters was a logical successive step. Fighter crew training began in 1951 and used tankers that were assigned to the bombardment wings. Proficiency developed rapidly and by mid-1952, fighters deploying to the Far East used air refueling between the West Coast and Hawaii.

On 20 January 1953, Headquarters SAC activated the 100th Air Refueling Squadron, Medium (20 UE KB-29P), at Turner AFB where it supported the fighter wings. It moved to Lockbourne on 20 May 1953. After the test period, five air refueling squadrons, strategic fighter, were activated in SAC. The first specifically designated fighter air refueling unit was the 506th Air Refueling Squadron which was activated at Dow AFB and assigned to the 506th Strategic Fighter Wing on 25 September 1953. The squadron UE was 20 KB-29P aircraft. For the next three months, one air refueling squadron, strategic fighter, was activated each month and assigned to one of the figher wings. On 20 October, the 27th Air Refueling Squadron was activated at Bergstrom AFB and assigned to the 27th Strategic Fighter Wing. On 24 November, the 100th Air Refueling Squadron, Medium, returned to Turner form Lockbourne. The next day it was inactivated, but the personnel and equipment were used to man and equip the 508th Air Refueling Squadron which was activated concurrently. The 407th Air Refueling Squadron was activated at Great Falls AFB on 18 December 1953 and assigned to the 407th Strategic Fighter Wing. Each of the four air refueling squadrons was activated with an aircraft authorization of 20 UE KB-29s.

The fifth squadron was the 71st Air Refueling Squadron, which was assigned to SAC, Eighth Air Force, and attached to the 506th Strategic Fighter Wing. It was activated at Dow AFB on 24 January 1955. It was the only such air refueling squadron equipped with 20 UE KC-97E aircraft. It was also the first KC-97 organization activated in the Eighth Air Force.

This tanker force of five squadrons for the strategic fighter wings was the peak strength. It was attained in January 1955, but by the middle of 1957 SAC's fighters had been inactivated or transferred to the Tactical Air Command. As a consequence, the two years from 1955 to 1957 was a period of many changes in the fighter tanker force.

Almost immediately after the activation of the last fighter air refueling squadron, organizational changes shifted assignments. Ten days after the activation of the 71st Air Refueling Squadron, the 506th Strategic Fighter Wing moved from Dow to Tinker AFB. Both air refueling squadrons remained at Dow, at least temporarily. Consequently, the 506th Air Refueling Squadron was relieved from assignment to the 506th Strategic Fighter Wing on 1 March 1955 and the 71st Air Refueling Squadron was relieved from attachment to the 506th on 8 March. Both squadrons were then assigned to the 4060th Air Refueling Wing and assigned to Second Air Force, 42nd Air Division, and attached to the 12th Strategic Fighter Wing and moved from Dow to Bergstrom.

Other changes were caused by the command reorganization of 1 April 1955. Among them, termination of fighter activities in the Eighth Air Force. When the 27th Strategic Fighter Wing was relieved from assignment to the Eighth Air Force and assigned to the Second Air Force, the 27th Air Refueling Squadron, Strategic Fighter, transferred with its parent wing.

The termination of the SAC fighters began in May 1956 and was completed a year later. On 11 May 1956, the 508th Strategic Fighter Wing at Turner AFB was inactivated. The 508th Air Refueling Squadron was relieved from assignment to the 508th Strategic Fighter Wing and assigned to the other fighter wing at Turner, the 31st Strategic Fighter Wing. On 1 April 1957, the 31st Strategic Fighter Wing was transferred from SAC to TAC and the 508th Air Refueling Squadron was relieved from assignment to the 31st Strategic Fighter Wing, Second Air Force, and assigned to the 4050th Air Refueling Wing, Eighth Air Force. The 4050th Air Refueling Wing was stationed at Westover AFB, but the 508th Air Refueling Squadron remained at Turner AFB. Ninety days later, on 1 July 1957, the 508th Air Refueling Squadron was inactivated.

Also on 1 July 1957, the 506th Air Refueling Squadron at Bergstrom AFB was inactivated. On the same date, the 407th Air Refueling Squadron, Strategic Fighter, was redesignated "Heavy" and reorganized with a 20 UE KC-97 table of organization. The only two remaining air refueling squadrons, strategic fighter, were the 27th and 71st. Although the 27th Strategic Fighter Wing was transferred to TAC on 1 July 1957, the 27th Air Refueling Squadron remained with SAC and the Second Air Force until 1 November 1957, when it was inactivated as the last KB-29 organization in the command. The 71st Air Refueling Squadron, Strategic Fighter, remained assigned to the 4060th Air Refueling Wing and was redesignated "Medium" on 15 December 1957.

Phasedown of SAC Fighters

The last fighter unit activated in SAC had been the 71st Strategic Reconnaissance Wing, Fighter. Even before this last unit was activated, Headquarters SAC had suggested a reduction in the fighter force. On 12 June 1954, Headquarters SAC proposed that the SAC fighter force be cut to two F-84F wings and one RF-84F wing. The reason behind this proposal was to gain facilities and personnel for the bomber and tanker expansion. The money saved by such elimination could be more gainfully used for the purchase of additional B-52s. Headquarters USAF was not responsive and decided no change would then be made in the SAC fighter force.

Later this was changed and phasedown of the SAC fighter force began when the high-priority 4080th Strategic Reconnaissance Wing, Light, was designated and organized on 1 May 1956 at Turner AFB. This assignment made Turner a three-wing base which was unmanageable. Shortly thereafter, on 11 May 1956, the 508th Strategic Fighter Wing was inactivated and the personnel and equipment were absorbed by the 4080th Strategic Reconnaissance Wing. Less than a year later on 1 April 1957, the 31st Strategic Fighter Wing, also stationed at Turner AFB, was

transferred to TAC. On 1 July 1957, the remaining five strategic
fighter wings in SAC were either inactivated or transferred to the
Tactical Air Command.

Fighter Missions in SAC

During the era of fighters assigned to the command, SAC's main
mission was to conduct intercontinental strategic bombing missions. In
addition, SAC was also assigned the mission to "train long-range fighter
crews and units for the performance of fighter, fighter-escort, and
joint Army and Navy operations." This October 1946 mission directive
provided guidance and an outline for the jobs that SAC fighters were to
accomplish. In this era, SAC took the lead in modern strategic warfare.
From 1946 to late 1952, SAC's fighter units had a primary and a secondary mission.

Primary Mission, 1946-1952. SAC's early war plans envisioned
deployment of bomber aircraft to forward operating bases in friendly
countries which would place the bombers closer to strategic targets in
Europe and Asia. As part of the plan, fighters were to deploy along
with the bombers and provide air defense of the forward bases and fly
escort missions for the bombers. On such missions, the fighters were to
protect bombers by serving as escorts to destroy hostile air defense
interceptors over enemy territory which were intent upon attacking and
destroying SAC's bombardment aircraft. A redesignation on 1 February
1950 reemphasized the primary mission of escort. On that date,
Headquarters SAC redesignated the 27th Fighter Wing, the group, and the
three figher squadrons "Fighter-Escort" units. Thus, the new name
reflected the stress placed on this part of the primary mission. The
other fighter wing in SAC at that time was not so redesignated. On 16
April 1950, the 1st Fighter Wing was redesignated "Fighter-Interceptor"
which was recognition of the limited escort capabilities of its UE
aircraft, F-86s.

The second part of the primary mission was to provide air
defense of the forward operating locations. This was tied in with the
SAC war plans which placed the bombers at these forward operating bases.
The figher mission required the fighter force to protect and defend the
friendly air bases from air attack and thereby protect the bomber
force. The primary mission remained unchanged until 1952 and 1953.

Secondary Missions, 1946-1957. The secondary mission for
SAC's fighter force initially consisted of two separate parts. The
first part directed the fighter to accomplish long-range offensive
intruder sorties to destroy hostile air forces on the ground or in area
defense. The second part called for fighter-bomber sorties in coopera-
tion with friendly ground forces. These close support missions were
historic in the assistance provided to the Army's ground forces by the
air forces. The secondary mission for SAC's fighter force was

expanded in 1950. Then, the mission was increased to include the air defense of important areas other than those specifically contained in the primary mission.

Between 1 July 1950 and 24 January 1953, three fighter wings were assigned to SAC, as well as four Air National Guard units. Each of the three regular units assigned to the command were either designated "Fighter-Escort" upon activation or they were redesignated "Fighter-Escort" shortly after assignment to SAC, as follows.

The 31st Fighter-Bomber Wing, 31st Fighter-Bomber Group, and teh 307th, 308th, and 309th Fighter-Bomber Squadrons were relieved form assignment to Continental Air Command and assigned to SAC on 1 July 1950. On 16 July, all units were redesignated "Fighter-Escort." On 1 November 1950, the 12th Fighter-Escort Wing, 12th Fighter-Escort Group, and the 559th 560th and 561st Fighter-Escort Squadrons were assigned to SAC and activated at Turner AFB. An identical action occurred on 1 July 1952 with the 508th Fighter-Escort Wing and its subordinate units. In this manner, one wing was redesignated upon reassignment and two were activated as "Fighter-Escort" wings. In conformity with these redesignations and activations, the 87th Fighter Group and the 535th Fighter Squadron, the USAFR Corollary units, had been redesignated "Fighter-Escort" units on 16 March 1950.

None of the Air National Guard units were ever redesignated as "Fighter-Escort" units. In recognition of the limitations of the UE aircraft performing escort missions, all four were redesignated "Fighter-Bomber" units in April, May, and June 1951.

Primary Mission, 1953-1957. In the early 1950s, scientific and technical developments permitted reduction in size and weight of atomic weapons. Miniaturization of components had reduced the overall weight and dimensions of the atomic bombs to the point where fighters could carry and deliver them. Furthermore, the size of fighters had steadily increased since 1945. For example, the F-101A (scheduled for delivery to SAC in 1954 and 1956) was only six feet shorter than the heavy bomber of World War II, the B-17H. Besides, the range of the fighter aircraft in SAC had been greatly extended by the practical application of air refueling.

As a logical development from the reduced size of atomic bombs, SAC expanded the primary mission of the fighters in 1953. This change caused the "fighter-escort" mission to give way to the delivery of nuclear weapons in support of the strategic offensive. The fighters in this manner were then considered part of the strategic striking force and were assigned Emergency War Plan (EWP) sorties and targets. SAC's strategic offensive concept was revised to include the requirement for the fighters to serve in a supportive role to assist in damage-limiting destruction of Soviet Union atomic weapon carriers. As a consequence, escort operations became secondary to the function of strategic strikes. The change in the mission and the revision of the offensive concept was a direct result of the reduced size of weapons and the increased size of the fighter aircraft.

Official designation recognized the mission change to atomic delivery on 20 January 1953, when all of SAC's fighter-escort units were redesignated strategic fighter wings and strategic fighter squadrons. Implementation of this conversion required the wings to achieve and maintain operational capability with atomic weapons. Aircraft had to be modified and crews trained in the new mission, with continuous refresher training to maintain proficiency. The fighter units in SAC retained this designation, with but one exception, until the fighter mission and units were phased out of the command.

Strategic Reconnaissance Wing, Fighter. The one exception to the standard designation of Strategic Fighter Wing for SAC's fighter units was the one with the primary mission of reconnaissance. This wing, the 71st Strategic Reconnaissance Wing, Fighter, was assigned to SAC from January 1955 to July 1957. Although the 71st was never considered in the role of an atomic weapon carrier, its mission was wider than other fighter wings because it conducted long-range strategic fighter reconnaissance as well as bombing and fighter-escort missions and maintained air refueling and mobility capabilities. In addition, the mission of one of its subordinate squadrons was augmented by a special mission. The 91st Strategic Reconnaissance Squadron, Fighter, was equipped with RF-84F aircraft and was part of the team for the parasite fighter conveyor (FICON) reconnaissance operations. When Headquarters USAF terminated the FICON program in February 1956, the primary mission of the squadron reverted to the original primary mission of the parent wing.

Fighter Operations

Fighter operations within SAC were devoted almost exclusively to training. the end product of the training program was aircrew combat readiness. Once attained, the training program was designed to maintain that proficiency.

The operational terms "mobility" and "combat readiness" were familiar ones throughout the command. Global training operations were carried out as part of the day-to-day routine. Although SAC combat fighter units were permanently stationed at bases in the United States, they regularly rotated to temporary duty stations at overseas bases.

The training program for SAC's long-range fighters began in 1946 along with the formation of the fighter units. In the initial stages, training encountered severe handicaps of reorganizations and shakedowns. There were manning shortages as the nation readjusted to a peacetime footing. In spite of the vast number of fighters produced through the war, there was an actual shortage of fighter aircraft until the fall of 1946. There were maintenance difficulties caused by lack of trained personnel compounded by shortages of supplies and equipment. Also, the P-51H fleet which comprised the SAC fighter force was grounded in late 1946 until modifications could be made to each aircraft.

Combat Readiness

There were many problems associated with maintaining a high state of readiness in the SAC fighter force. In fact, combat readiness in the fighter units seldom attained the status desired. For the SAC fighter units, combat readiness status (as of 31 December) was as follows:

	1946	1947	1948	1949	1950	1951	1952	1953	1954	1955	1956	1957
Assigned Units	3	5	2	2	3	3	4	6	6	7	6	0
Combat Ready	0	0	2	2	2	0	1	4	0	2	3	0

The "zero" combat readiness rating on 31 December 1946 was caused by the fact that only one unit was fully activated and equipped with aircraft. The two others were not equipped. the one active and equipped unit, the 56th Fighter Group, had been organized only for a short period of time and did not even receive its official aircraft until September 1946. In 1947 the 4th and 56th Fighter Groups were converting to a new and tactically untried aircraft, the P-80A. The 27th and 82nd had only been activated in August and June, respectively, and were in the process of starting the training program at the end of the year. The fifth fighter unit, the 33rd Fighter Group, had only been activated since early September and was not combat ready.

The "zero" combat readiness rating for the fighter units on 31 December 1951 was caused by a shortage of aircraft. This, in turn, was caused by the delivery of aircraft from production lines consistently falling behind delivery schedules. Consequently, progress to combat readiness status was retarded. The aircraft delivery slippage extended over into 1952 as well. The "zero" combat readiness rating for the fighter units on 31 December 1954 was the result of the conversion program that replaced the F-84G with F-84F aircraft. The first F-84F aircraft was received by SAC in January 1954, but engine problems with these first conversions led to a major engine modification program. The first F-84F with the improved engines arrived on 18 June 1954. None of the six fighter wings was combat ready until 1955. The first three wings attained combat readiness on 1 April, the next two on 1 May, and the sixth on 1 November 1955. By the end of the year, a reversal occurred. Only two wings, the 407th and 506th Strategic Fighter Wings, still retained combat readiness. Additional problems with the engines had caused the others to lose that status.

At the end of 1956, the number of fighter wings had been reduced because the 508th Strategic Fighter Wing had been inactivated on 11 May 1956. The three combat-ready units were the 31st, 407th, and 506th Strategic Fighter Wings. The 27th Strategic Fighter Wing was in the process of converting to F-101As and, therefore, was not combat ready. The other unit was the 12th Strategic Fighter Wing which was noncombat ready at the end of the year.

In 1957 the five strategic fighter wings were either inactivated or transferred to TAC. SAC's one strategic reconnaissance wing, fighter, was inactivated. Units had gradually phased down from combat readiness status starting in February 1957.

Combat readiness for the air refueling squadrons that supported the fighters was never a problem. These units were activated in late 1953 and were equipped with KB-29Ps. One KC-97E squadron was activated in 1955. The fighter air refueling squadrons were activated upon the inactivation of a bomber air refueling squadron and personnel and equipment were assigned to the fighter refueling unit. Thus, all were combat ready from time of activation until the end of the squdrons in 1957.

Readiness for the fighters was hampered by several physical problems. For example, in the early days of jet engines there were not many bases that stocked jet fuel. Consequently, training flight plans had to be prepared and filed, not on the basis of the type of training necessary but to be sure that adquate jet fuel was available. The early shortage of experienced jet mechanics was even more critical. Physical features also included the nature and adequacy of the base. The 27th Fighter-Escort Wing moved from Kearney AFB to Bergstrom AFB because the facilities at Kearney were inadequate. Later, the 506th Strategic Fighter Wing moved from Dow AFB to Tinker AFB because the runway at Dow was too short for the F-84F aircraft. Combat readiness dropped with each move.

Combat readiness was also directly affected by the aircraft conversion program. As each new type of aircraft was assigned, the process of attaining a high state of readiness had to start over from the beginning. As a consequence, the state of readiness in SAC fighter wings fluctuated with the conversion program. For example, as mentioned above, Dow AFB was adequate for the F-84G, but not for the F-84F.

During the expansion of the Air Force in the 1950s, combat ready units were stripped down to form a cadre of personnel to provide manpower for new organizations. For example, the activation of a second fighter wing at Turner AFB (508th Fighter-Escort Wing) on 1 July 1952 affected the 31st Fighter-Escort Wing also stationed there. Until 1 July, the 31st had been able to maintain effective manning and combat readiness of personnel at nearly 90 percent. Then, when some combat

24

ready crews were transferred to the 508th, the 31st suffered. Until both units could attain the desired level of readiness, they were rated noncombat ready.

An additional feature affecting combat readiness was the fact that several SAC units deploying to overseas locations left their aircraft and equipment in place for the rotational replacement. When the unit returned without its aircraft, it needed complete reequipping. Until this was accomplished, the unit had no combat readiness.

Fighter Flight Training*

Combat readiness depended upon an effective training program. The variety of missions assigned to SAC's fighter force caused the fighter crews to engage in many different types of training. Overall, the training program remained stable through the years but was augmented with the important additions of training for inflight refueling in late 1951 and for delivery of nuclear weapons in 1953 and 1954.

The factors that affected combat readiness hand an equal impact on training proficiency. Periodic shortages of aircraft, limited allocations of flying hours, and the entire effect of rotations resulted in reduced training programs. The training programs were complicated and, exclusive of transition training for new pilots, the different types of training were conducted simultaneously.

The types of training that were stable throughout the program were as follows:

Primary Mission

Simulated Combat Sorties, Fighter to Fighter	- Escort
Simulated Combat Sorties, Fighter to Bomber	- Defense
High Altitude Aerial Gunnery, Live Rounds	- Escort and Defense
Low Altitude Aerial Gunnery, Live Rounds	- Escort and Defense
Camera Gunnery, High Altitude	- Escort and Defense
Camera Gunnery, Low Altitude	- Escort and Defense
Cruise Control	- Escort

---

* This section excludes long-range and overseas deployments and rotations of SAC fighter units. These flights by their dramatic nature and inclusive subject matter merit separate attention and are discussed in "Overseas Deployments and Rotations."

Secondary Missions

Ground Gunnery	- Ground Support
Dive Bombing	- Ground Support
Rocketry	- Ground Support

In 1946, fighter training was limited to the 56th Fighter Group because it was the only unit equipped with aircraft. As soon as the P-51Hs began to arrive in June 1946, flight training for the unit began at Selfridge. In the same month, Headquarters SAC had formulated plans for the 56th to fly to Alaska on deployment for Arctic experience in conjunction with a very heavy bombardment group.[*] As a consequence of SAC's plan, the 56th Fighter Group undertook a training program for the deployment and for Arctic indoctrination.

Even though the entire group had undertaken Arctic indoctrination, only one squadron, the 62nd Fighter Squadron, Single Engine, flew to Alaska for operational testing. While there, the 62nd conducted familiarization flights, gunnery practice, and tested Arctic navigation. Little opportunity existed for fighter escort training operations with the B-29s of the 28th Bombardment Group, Very Heavy.

Expansion of SAC's fighter units and modernization of the aircraft in 1947 produced a substantial increase in training for the escort, defense, and ground support missions of the fighters. One of the most significant was the training program for the new jet fighter, the P-80A.

The first P-80A arrived at Selfridge in April 1947 and was assigned to the 56th Fighter Group. The first exercises conducted with this aircraft were demonstration flights. On 9 June 1947, 12 P-80s over-flew Chicago and Lake Michigan. At that time, it was the largest demonstration flight of jet aircraft. In August, 36 P-80s were assembled for the same type of flight over Pontiac, Port Huron, and Detroit, again representing the largest force of jets ever assembled. The demonstrations were showpieces and the serious training began in late August.

The first experience that the 56th obtained in its primary mission of escort with P-80s occurred in August 1947 when it flew six missions in conjunction with B-29 bombers. These missions were flown

---

[*] The original bomber group scheduled to deploy to Alaska was the 449th, but it was inactivated on 4 August 1946. The 28th Bombardment Group, Very Heavy, from Grand Island AAF, Nebraska, went to Alaska in September 1946 and returned in April 1947.

by the 61st Fighter Squadron, Jet, and conducted on a ratio of two P-80s to one B-29. Additional similar experience followed the next month. During bombing maneuvers at Wendover, Utah, six P-80s flew joint operations with the bombardment units. The fighters flew dual missions: escort, and then they would turn and conduct attack and interception missions. The bombers were flown at 25,000 to 29,000-feet altitude. The main purposes of these flights were to compute fuel consumption at escort altitudes and speeds and to test the P-80 against the B-29. The conclusion was that these missions were very successful, but the fighter squadron reported that little training was obtained by its crews.

These tests and exercises were not systematic, and in October 1947 more thorough tests of the combat suitability of the new jet fighter were conducted at Fort Worth AAF, Texas. The 63rd Fighter Squadron, Jet, flew eight P-80s from Selfridge for a series of escort and interception evaluation missions against B-29s. These missions produced conclusions that the P-80, flying at 36,000 feet and using 110-gallon wing tip tanks, could successfully escort a B-29 for 425 miles. Tactically, weaving back and forth over the flight path of the much slower B-29 was a better technique than reducing speed to that of the bomber and flying a parallel course. For the interception part of the tests, the fighter equipped with wing tip tanks could best make a head-on attack. Without such tanks, attack from any angle was possible. Interception range without tanks was 200 miles; with tanks, it was extended to 350 miles.

Upon conclusion of these missions, many questions remained unanswered. In November, Headquarters SAC requested additional tests to obtain further data, specifically on personal equipment of the P-80 pilot, on the problems of transition training from piston-engined fighters to jets, om maintenance requirements, fuel consumption, and service-ability. These tests occupied the two P-80 groups for the remainder of the year.

As in 1946, the fighter operations throughout 1947 were confined largely within the 56th Fighter Group. The newly-activated groups were not ready for full-fledged operations.

Once these units were fully equipped, the tempo of training acitivites increased. By July 1948, three units had progressed sufficiently to be subjected to operational readiness tests which were designed to evaluate the units. Out of a possible 990 points for fighter units, the 56th scored highest with 853, the 4th followed with 825, and the 33rd scored 771. Some points lost by the 33rd were caused by events outside its control, such as bad weather and inadequate facilities for gunnery.

Further evidence of the increased tempo of training was obvious by deployment to forward bases by fighter units.* Additional evidence occurred with the SAC maximum effort bombing and fighter interception missions. On 7 January 1948, a maximum effort exercise occurred. Fighter units were able to get 107 of 117 P-80s into the air and 186 of 224 P-51s. Another maximum effort exercise was conducted at Selfridge AFB on 2 June 1948. Eighth Air Force units launched 213 aircraft and 191 were effective over the target. The 191 effectives included 112 fighters of the 27th and 33rd Fighter Wings. During this operation, the 27th escorted bombers from Kansas City to Bloomington, Illinois, at which point the 33rd assumed escort responsibilities to Selfridge.

The Eighth Air Force launched similar attacks against Amarillo and Kansas City in May 1948. The bombers attacked in formation and the camera bombing occurred at 20,000 feet. Fighters from the 27th and 33rd Fighter Wings accompanied the bombers on both missions. One recommendation for the fighters that came from these exercises was that the fighter aircraft be equipped with wing tip tanks for long-range missions. Additional fighter training missions in 1948 were routine gunnery training and exercises with the Air Defense Command (ADC) at McChord AFB.

The range tests of the P-80 in October 1947 had proved it inadequate for EWO escort. The two P-80 wings, the 4th and 56th, were reassigned to the Continental Air Command for air defense on 1 December 1948. The third jet unit, the P-84B-equipped 33rd Fighter Wing, was also reassigned to the same command on the same date. As a result, SAC was left with only two fighter units, 27th and 82nd, both equipped with piston-engined aircraft.

On 1 May 1949, the 1st Fighter Wing, primarily an air defense unit equipped with F-86A, was assigned to SAC. The three fighter wings assigned to SAC participated in three major defense maneuvers with Continental Air Command. Two, Blackjack and Lookout, concerned the defense of the Northeast section of the nation. The third, Overgreasy, concentrated its efforts on the Northwest. In these exercises, SAC fighters often provided assistance to the defense forces, while SAC bombers filled the role of attackers. The original concept was to have the fighters fly maximum effort escort missions. The concept changed before they were executed and in none of these exercises was SAC permitted to give the defense system a realistic test. As a result, SAC participation became only incidental. SAC fighters flew no escort missions in the Northeast. In fact, the 82nd Fighter Wing flew predetermined relays with its F-51s for practice sorties to be used by Ground Control Intercept (GCI) personnel. These exercises had become aircraft warning

---

* See section, "Deployments and Rotations."

28

and air raid defense operations. In the Northwest, the 71st Fighter Squadron of the 1st Fighter Wing used its F-86s to assist the defenders in attacking the offensive forces of B-29s and B-50s.

Differences of effectiveness were reported in this exercise. The 93rd Bombardment Wing had flown 10 sorties in the Northwest operation. Crews reported that few interceptions were made. The 71st Fighter Squadron crews reported that coordinated attacks by F-86s could prove effective against any bomber encountered in this exercise, up to 35,000 feet altitude.

The hectic fluctuations of units and aircraft in the SAC fighter program in the first four years caused instability in training. This was changed in 1950 and the training program improved. One feature was the beginning of a long period of assignment of F-84s. Pilot transition from one F-84 model to another was easier than transition from one type aircraft to another.

Training progress was evident in the 27th Fighter-Escort Wing which became a test unit for the F-84E. A significant number of aircraft did not arrive until March 1950. There were delays in delivery, but after six months of training, crews of the 27th ferried 180 F-84Es to Europe in two increments (see section, "Ocean Crossings, Atlantic"). By November 1950, it was the most experienced F-84E wing in SAC and was selected for deployment to Korea to engage in combat. It returned in July 1951, with several months' combat experience. In addition, SAC's fighter crew training was also improved by stressing escort and interception for all types of bombers and even including the jet-engined RB-45 of the 91st Strategic Reconnaissance Wing. Escort missions were flown during which escort tactics and techniques were developed and tested. In some instances, when bombers were not available for escort practice, F-84 aircraft simulated bombers in order that training could continue. Training of this sort did much to advance the efficiency of SAC's fighters and crews.

In September and October 1951, the first F-84G fighters were assigned to the 27th and 31st Fighter-Escort Wings. The F-84G represented improvements over the F-84E in that they could be refueled in the air with the boom refueling method. This increased training requirements because crews had to attain proficiency in refueling. Consequently, an intensive inflight refueling training program for all fighter pilots was undertaken.

Inflight refueling training began in January 1952. It proved to be a success from the beginning. Both fighter and tanker crews acquired proficiency in a short period of time. For the remainder of the service of fighters in SAC, the level of success in this technique remained high.

In 1953, the mission change assigning atomic capability to SAC's fighter wings increased the training requirements. The initial stages of training were delayed because of a slippage in the program supplying bomb delivery equipment. This specialized equipment began arriving on the fighter bases in June 1953 and by September all were equipped. Pilots were required to complete bomb commander school and then participate in applicable flying training to increase individual proficienty.

Periodically, the training program encountered obstacles that caused setbacks. Aircraft availability frequently was one obstacle in that shortages increased the crew ratio and reduced monthly flying time. Even such an instance as the oil strike in the spring of 1952 caused a reduction in the flying hours with a resultant impact on training.

The Air National Guard and USAF Reserve Corollary units in SAC encountered extensive training difficulties in association with SAC standards. While these five units were assigned to SAC, their training accomplishments and proficiency were not such that they ever attained the fully-qualified level. Many factors contributed to this consistent deficiency. In the case of officer and airman manning, the required level of 90 percent effective manning in both categories was never reached by any of the five units for the entire period. In the area of aircraft possession, the only unit of the five to possess the full complement of UE aircraft was the 108th Fighter-Bomber Wing. Since it was equipped with F-47Ds, there was no shortage of this type. None of the other units which were equipped with F-51 and F-84 aircraft ever attained the full complement and usually hovered around the 60 percent mark. For those aircraft that each unit did possess, the SAC in-commission goal was 80 percent. Even the 108th Fighter-Bomber Wing with its full complement of assigned aircraft reached this level only during the month of September 1951. The F-51s of the 132nd and 146th Fighter-Bomber Wings were rated at 98 and 85 percent, respectively, for two weeks in April 1951, immediately upon assignment to SAC. After those initial weeks, the rate dropped to a realistic average of about 50 percent in-commission.

Long-Range and Overseas Deployments

One of the most important training efforts was the deployment of SAC fighters to distant and overseas bases. From the first months in the history of the command, aircraft and personnel deployed to advanced bases in Alaska, Europe, Asia, and North Africa. These deployments later developed into systematic rotations. They placed the aircraft closer to targets. Rotations acquainted crews with foreign base potential in case they should be required to use them at a later date under war conditions. In addition, deployment and redeployment served as mobility training missions. Furthermore, while on these temporary duty (TDY) rotations, fighter crews trained along with the bomber crews, performed air defense missions, and, in the case of the Korean War, engaged in combat operations. The training was similar to that conducted at the home bases.

Fighter units in SAC occupied only a few bases as home stations in comparison with the bomber units. The two main fighter bases were Turner and Bergstrom AFBs. At the peak strength of seven fighter wings, in January 1955 through 11 May 1956, four wings were located at these two bases. the other three wings were located at Larson, Malmstrom, and Tinker AFBs. However, this listing would create a false impression of the global distribution of the fighters which deployed to advanced bases in the same manner as the bombers. In most instances of fighter deployment, they were used in their secondary mission of air defense. This remained valid whether only a part of the unit or the whole unit deployed. Regardless, some of these operations were pioneering ventures with sufficient merit to bring significant awards and trophies. The first deployments were North America to Alaska.

North America -- Alaska. The first long-range temporary duty (TDY) of a SAC fighter unit was the deployment of the 62nd Fighter Squadron, Single Engine. This squadron, a subordinate unit of the 56th Fighter Group, Single Engine, had been activated at Selfridge Army Air Field, Michigan, on 1 May 1946, the first fighter unit in SAC. In August, the 62nd Fighter Squadron was notified that it would be placed on TDY for six months to Alaska sometime in November. The timing of the notification caused some difficulty because, although the group had been substantially manned since the end of May, no aircraft had been assigned until June when the first six P-51H aircraft of an authorized 75 arrived. By the end of September, the number had increased to 57 but the full authorization was not attained until the end of October 1946.

In preparation for the TDY, not only the 62nd Fighter Squadron but also all the units of the 56th Fighter Group underwent extensive Arctic indoctrination courses. The ground echelon of the squadron (ten officers and 217 enlisted men) departed Selfridge AAF on 20 November 1946. In contrast to later deployments by advance parties and ground echelons by air transport, this ground echelon used water and rail transportation en route. On 18 December 1946, 28 P-51H aircraft departed Selfridge AAF and flew to Ladd AAF (see map, next page), arriving ten days later. three B-29s accompanied the flight to carry spare parts, tools, and maintenance personnel. The 62nd Fighter Squadron was scheduled to engage in Arctic training for six months, but it came back in April 1947, because the 56th Fighter Group, Single Engine, was redesignated the 56th Fighter Group, Jet-Propelled, and was thus in the process of conversion from P-51Hs to P-80As, jet-propelled fighter aircraft. This abbreviated rotation of a SAC fighter unit to Alaska was the first of many such rotations.

Keflavik

Fairbank

Big Delta

Bluie West One

Whitehors

Goose

Fort Nelson

reat Falls

Grenier

Otis

Rapid City

Selfridge

McGuire

Chanute McCook

Tinker

Turner

Bergstrom

18 December 1946. 28 P-51Hs of the 62d Fighter Squadron of the 56th Fighter Group left Selfridge AAF to fly to Ladd Field near Fairbanks, Alaska. They arrived on 28 December 1946 and remained there until April 1947.

On 1 April 1948, the 82d Fighter Wing began deployment to Ladd Field. The three squadrons departed with one-day separation and the last aircraft landed at Ladd Field on 17 April 1948.

The next unit deployed to the Arctic was the 82nd Fighter Wing, Single Engine, stationed at Grenier AFB, New Hampshire. On this occasion, all three fighter squadrons deployed. The TDY move began on 1 April 1948 when 21 F-51H aircraft of the 96th Fighter Squadron, Single Engine, left Grenier AFB for Ladd AFB, Alaska (see map on preceding page). The other two squadrons, the 95th and 97th, left two days later. Total elapsed time for the 96th Fighter Squadron was 11 days because weather had forced delays of two days at Chanute AFB, Illinois, and eight days at Whitehorse in the Yukon Territory (YT). One aircraft crashed en route. The 95th Fighter Squadron also required 11 days to make the trip, but its weather delay occurred at Big Delta AFB, Alaska. Two aircraft crashed in emergency landings at Whitehorse, YT. The third squadron, the 97th, encountered greater difficulties en route. One aircraft crashed at Whitehorse, YT. Weather delays at Great Falls (Malmstrom) AFB, Montana, at Fort Nelson, Canada, at Whitehorse, YT, and at Big Delta AFB, Alaska, kept the unit from arriving at Ladd AFB until 17 April 1948.

Although this TDY was also scheduled for six months, it, too, was shortened. On 20 June 1948, flying training operations were terminated with the purpose of readying the aircraft for the return to Grenier AFB. Departure dates were staggered from 27 to 30 June 1948. Forty-nine F-51Hs flew back to Grenier AFB by retracing the deployment routes. The Canadian government had objected to large formations of aircraft using the north-south route and, as a result, formations of the 82nd Fighter Wing were limited to flight size. Forty-seven aircraft completed the return flight without incident. Two aircraft were forced to land and required engine changes before making it back to Grenier AFB.

In September 1948, the 4th Fighter Wing, stationed at Andrews AFB, Maryland, was scheduled to begin its Arctic indoctrination. Before action could be taken, an organizational change relieved SAC of responsibility for this unit. On 1 December 1948, the 4th Fighter Wing was relieved from assignment to SAC and assigned to the Continental Air Command. Had this wing been deployed north, it would have been the first SAC jet fighter unit to be deployed to Alaska. Instead, SAC jet fighter unit deployment waited for several years.

Strategic fighter aircraft deployment to Alaska resumed in 1955. As a part of the expanded USAF air defense effort, Eielson AFB (near Fairbanks) and Elmendorf AFB (near Anchorage), Alaska, were added to the SAC sphere of fighter wing rotational activity. SAC's requirement was to maintain a fighter detachment of squadron strength supported by air refueling tankers in Alaska at all times. The command arranged a 90-day rotational schedule that remained active until the fighters were terminated in SAC on 1 July 1957. Furthermore, since the Eighth Air Force was not concerned with fighters after 1 April 1955, the mission fell to the fighter units of the Second Air Force and to one wing of the Fifteenth Air Force. Deployments were as follows:

Unit	Dates	Air Force
508th SFW	Aug–Nov 55	2nd
506th SFW	Nov 55–Feb 56	2nd
407th SFW	Feb–May 56	15th
12th SFW	May–Aug 56	2nd
506th SFW	Aug–Nov 56	2nd
31st SFW	Nov 56–Feb 57	2nd
407th SFW	Feb–May 57	15th
506th SFW	May–Jul 57	2nd

Air refueling technology made vast changes in the deployments. In the early years, the fighters followed flight plans that had them land at many bases en route. In the new era, the fighter squadron launched from the home base, was refueled, and then landed at Great Falls AFB, (later renamed Malmstrom) Montana. They would leave the next day and with one air refueling in Canada arrive at the Alaska base that evening. Redeployment was nonstop with several refuelings en route. The 407th SFW, already stationed at Malmstrom AFB, flew direct on its deployments in 1955 and 1957. In 1957, the 506th SFW, stationed at Tinker AFB, Oklahoma, flew direct, nonstop both going to and coming from Eielson AFB.

On 1 July 1957, all rotations of SAC fighter wings to Alaska terminated along with the end of fighters in the command.

North America -- Caribbean. To provide training in overwater flying and long-range navigation, Headquarters SAC had considered deployments into the Caribbean. USAF authority was requested for flights of fighters into Ramey AFB, Puerto Rico, Kindley AFB, Bermuda, and Vernam AFB, Jamaica in 1948. The request proposed a direct flight nonstop from the United States, but landing permission was asked for refueling at Oakes Field, Bermuda. Headquarters USAF approved the request for the operation with two deviations: Albrook AFB, Canal Zone was added and Oakes Field permission was denied.

Headquarters SAC scheduled the 4th and 56th Fighter Wings for the Caribbean deployment with the 4th Fighter Wing pioneering the route. The flights were to start in May, not more than eight aircraft were to be sent at one time, and overflight of independent nations in the area was prohibited.

Survey of the route by the 4th Fighter Wing raised questions about the flight. In a report of the survey, the wing requested a delay until mid-June to provide adequate weather reconnaissance information. Without it, the wing recommended abandoning the Bermuda flight. It considered it an uncertain gamble since it was a maximum range flight for the F-80 with no alternate bases; unfavorable headwinds could reduce the maximum range, and failure of components* in the F-80 could cost the life of the pilot and the aircraft.

Regardless, these flights were carried out in May and June 1948. On 24 May, the 56th Fighter Wing sent four P-80A aircraft first to MacDill AFB, Florida, and then overwater to Jamaica and back without incident. In early June, the 4th Fighter Wing sent four P-80s from Andrews AFB, Maryland, to Jamaica and the Canal Zone, again without incident. In late June, the 4th Fighter Wing sent four aircraft to Bermuda. Despite apprehension over this flight, the fighters flew direct to Kindley AFB. The conclusions and recommendations of the flight leaders were in direct opposition to the purpose originally justifying the flights. None reported that these flights were beneficial for training purposes.

A much larger fighter deployment to the Caribbean provided for 50 F-82 aircraft of the 27th Fighter Group to fly from the home base at Kearney AFB, Nebraska, to Howard AFB, Panama, and return. Refueling and maintenance stops were to be made at MacDill AFB, Florida, and Ramey AFB, Puerto Rico, on the way south. On the return flight, stops were to be made at Vernam AFB, Jamaica, and Carswell AFB, Texas. Three C-47s carried spare parts and maintenance personnel. The mass flight began when 55 of the F-82s took off from Kearney AFB on 1 February 1949. Due to a one-day layover at MacDill AFB and Ramey AFB, the flight arrived at Howard AFB on 5 February with 11 aborts en route. On 8 February the flight departed Howard AFB for Vernam AFB and remained overnight, leaving the next day for Carswell AFB. Several of the aborted aircraft rejoined the flight on the return and 49 F-82s landed at Kearney AFB on 10 February 1949.

In contrast to the final reports from the 4th and 56th Fighter Groups, the conclusion to the deployment of the 27th was that the flight proved to be valuable for flying personnel. It also proved the feasibility of long-range flights using dead reckoning and celestial navigation. Invaluable supply and maintenance experience showed that ground crews could do the job if they were given adequate rest. Pilots also developed a confidence factor as noted in the final report: "Most certainly those individuals who had never flown over water in fighters are now convinced that such flights are nothing less than everyday routine if proper planning is accomplished."

Ocean Crossings -- Atlantic. SAC's golbal mission of strategic bombing required that the command's fighters cross the Atlantic Ocean to bases in Europe. In some ways, the Caribbean flights involving SAC fighters were preliminaries to the longer oceanic crossings. While

---

* Loss of oxygen, main fuel pump, or electrical generator would force the F-80 to land immediately or crash.

the Caribbean flights were taking place, planning was underway for flights across the Atlantic Ocean.

There were two routes used for crossing the Atlantic Ocean, both of which followed the ferry routes used by the Air Transport Command during World War II. The first of these was the Northern Route. Here, the aircraft would usually leave from a northern state base, preferably Bangor, Maine, and fly to the first stop at Goose Bay, Labrador. From there, the fighters would proceed to Bluie West One (Narsarssuak), Greenland, and then to one of the airfields in Iceland. The longest leg of the journey was from Iceland to Prestwick, Scotland. After Prestwick, the fighters could deploy to almost any base in the United Kingdom and then to Europe. The major difficulties with this route were the unfavorable weather conditions encountered, the limited navigational aids, and the fact that there were no alternate airfields after Goose Bay. Yet this was the most direct route to England and was gradually improved over the years.

The second route for crossing the Atlantic was the Central Route, the most direct route to bases in North Africa. This route started from an eastern United States base such as Turner AFB, Georgia. The first leg of the flight would be to Kindley AFB, Bermuda. The second leg was to Lajes Field in the Azores. The last leg was the longest overwater from the Azores to Nouasseur, Morocco.

When air refueling techniques were developed and perfected for use by the fighters, the flights were made directly to the overseas bases. But until that time, the aircraft had to stage through these bases in the crossings of the Atlantic Ocean.

The first Atlantic Ocean crossing was Fox Able One (fighter, Atlantic) undertaken by 16 F-80s of the 56th Fighter Wing, stationed at Selfridge AFB, Michigan. The 56th wing commander proposed this move in February 1948. He justified it on the basis that it would ". . . provide experience and information for future planning in the movement of the P-80 type aircraft over long distances for tactical purposes." The proposed route followed the Northern Atlantic course starting at Bangor, Maine, and ending at Bovington, England. The proposal itemized the requirements for seven support aircraft. Four C-47s would be needed for spare parts and maintenance personnel. Two B-17s would be required for air-sea rescue, and one B-29 would be necessary for weather reconnaissance as well as serving as a pace aircraft. Estimated flying time for the F-80s was placed at 17 hours.

The 16 F-80s departed Selfridge AFB on 14 July 1948 (see map, next page). This historic flight was accomplished according to plan without a major operational or mechanical problem. While in England, the wing detachment made a side flight to Furstenfeldbruck (Munich), Germany. The completion of this deployment proved the feasibility of sending jet fighters to European bases under their own power.

36

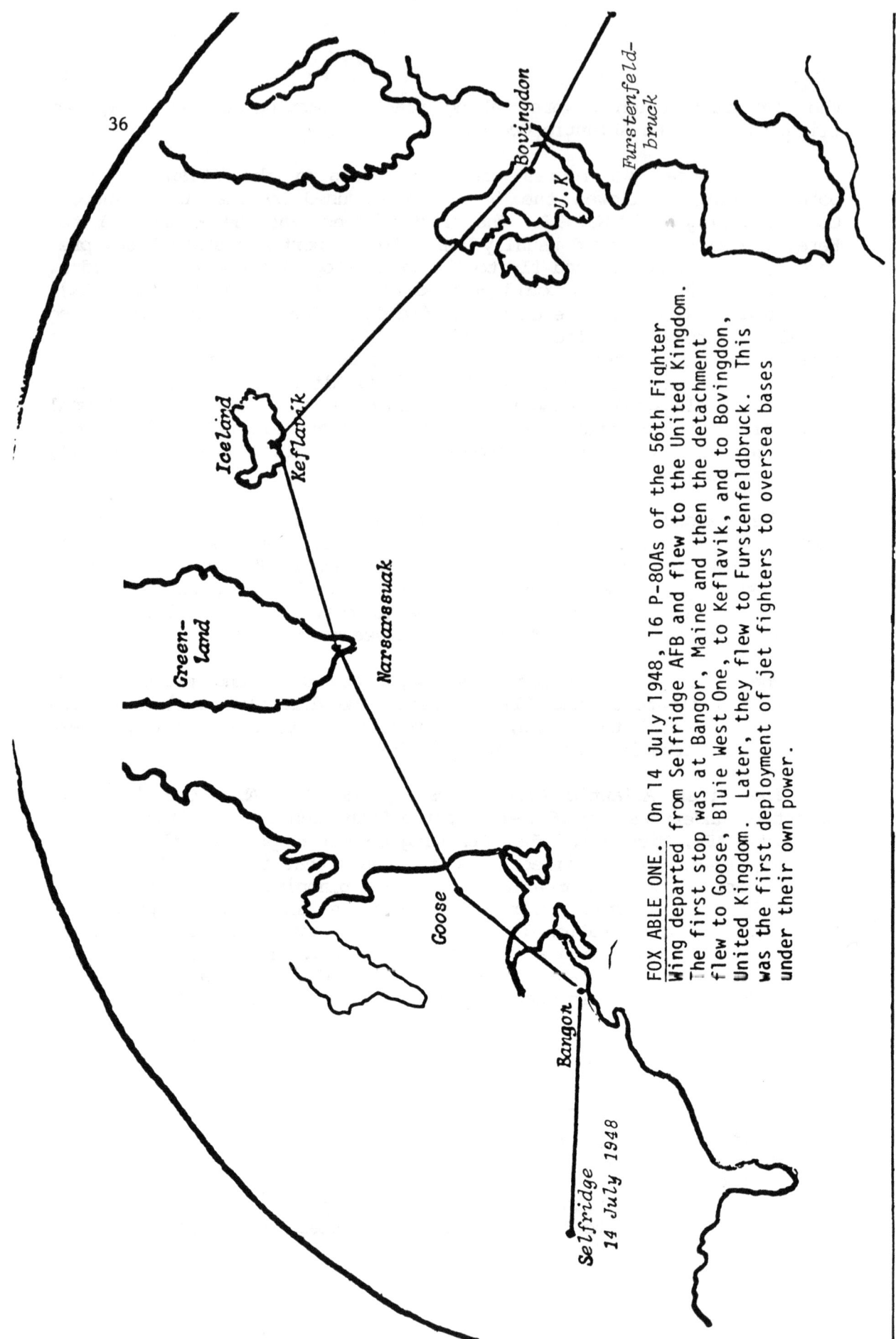

FOX ABLE ONE. On 14 July 1948, 16 P-80As of the 56th Fighter Wing departed from Selfridge AFB and flew to the United Kingdom. The first stop was at Bangor, Maine and then the detachment flew to Goose, Bluie West One, to Keflavik, and to Bovingdon, United Kingdom. Later, they flew to Furstenfeldbruck. This was the first deployment of jet fighters to oversea bases under their own power.

Selfridge
14 July 1948

Bangor

Goose

Narsarssuak

Green-
land

Iceland

Keflavik

Bovingdon

U.K.

Furstenfeld-
bruck

One of the most significant Atlantic crossings by SAC fighter units was Fox Able Three (see map on following page). For this mission, pilots of the 27th FEW were required to ferry 180 F-84E aircraft from Bergstrom AFB to air bases in Germany. Prior to the flights, pilots had to pick up 262 F-84Es from the Republic Aviation factory on Long Island, New York, and fly them to Bergstrom for shakedown flights. Then, 180 of those aircraft had to be ferried overseas in two increments and delivered to the 36th and 86th Fighter-Bomber Groups. The movements took place in September and October 1950.

Ninety F-84Es of the first increment departed Bergstrom on 15 September. One aircraft experienced hydraulic difficulties and returned to Bergstrom. The remaining 89 followed the northern route across the Atlantic from McGuire AFB to Goose AB, to Bluie West One, to Keflavik AB, to Manston RAF Station, to Furstenfeldbruck AB, Germany. The trip took three days for the 5,858 miles and was without incident. The pilots were returned by Military Air Transport Service to Bergstrom on 24 September.

The second increment included the remaining 90 aircraft plus the one that had aborted. They departed Bergstrom on 15 October and arrived in Germany on 28 October. They followed the same route as the first group, but bad weather forced delays all along the route.

Each one of these flights represented the largest mass flight of fighter aircraft to Europe up to that time. In the case of the first one, it was accomplished in the shortest time up to that point. For successfully planning and executing this ferrying mission, the 27th FEW was awarded the MacKay Trophy for 1950.

The outstanding success of Fox Able Three was followed by Fox Able Ten. On the day after Christmas 1950, 74 F-84Es and four T-33s of the 31st Fighter-Escort Wing took off from Turner AFB en route to Manston, England (see map on second following page). The F-84s stopped at Otis AFB for refueling while the T-33s landed at Andrews AFB. The next leg of the flight took them to Goose AB where bad weather stalled the deployment for two days. When the weather cleared, the flight resumed and the aircraft landed at Bluie West One in Greenland. From there, they flew to Keflavik, Iceland, refueled, and then flew to England, landing at several bases there. By 6 January 1951, all F-84s and two of the T-33s were in place at Manston, England. One T-33 aborted at Goose and had to return to Turner for repairs. The other T-33 crashed at Bluie West One. During Fox Able Ten, the tactical aircraft had been accompanied by six MATS C-54Ds and one SAC C-54 carrying personnel and supplies. Two of the C-54s operated in a "leapfrog" mode to arrive at the bases ahead of the tactical aircraft. The seventh C-54 covered the weather reconnaissance and air control function. The 31st FEW remained on overseas duty in England, executing flights to the continent and to Norway, until late July 1951. Then all aircraft remained at Manston, England, where the 12th FEW, the

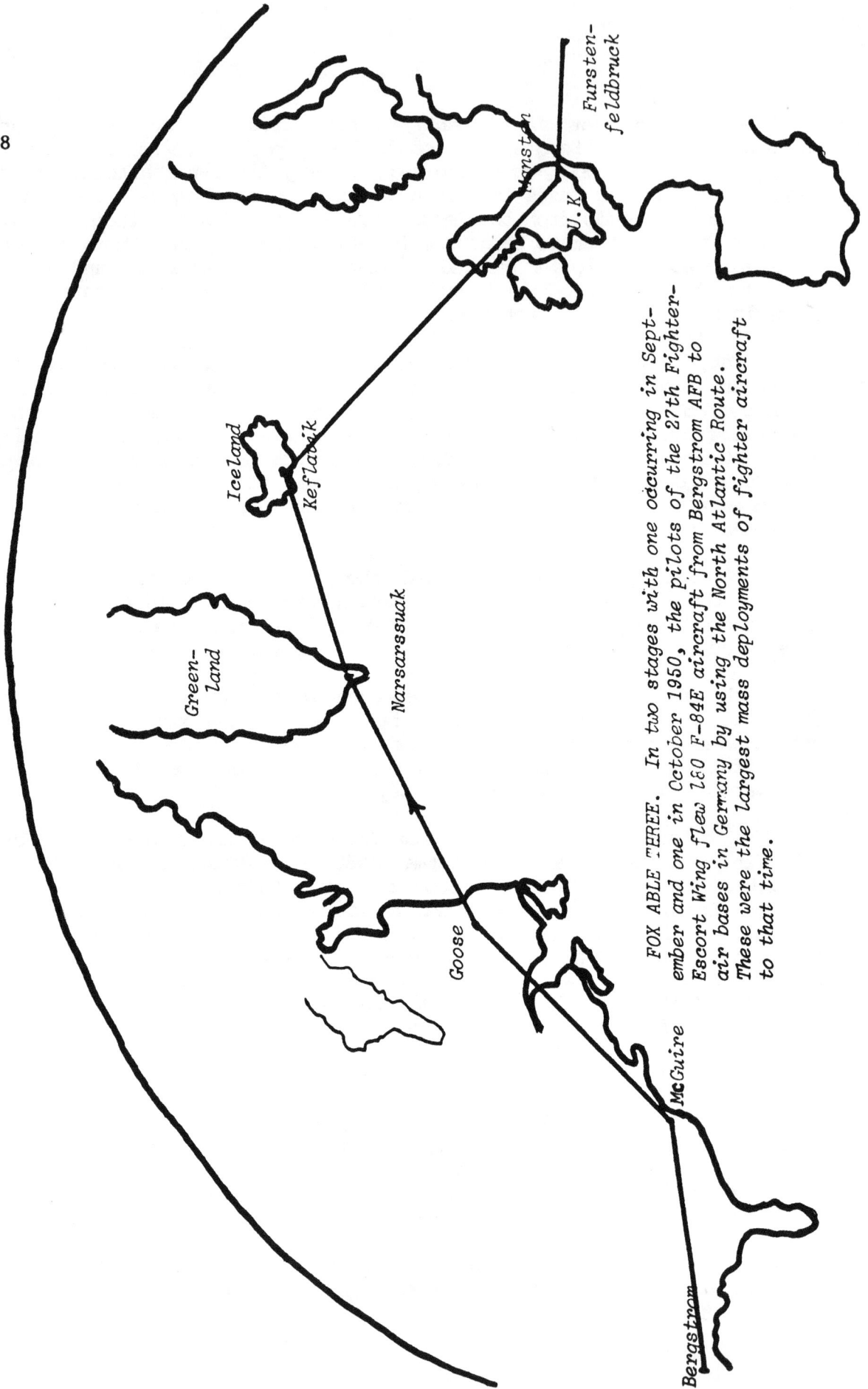

FOX ABLE THREE. In two stages with one occurring in September and one in October 1950, the pilots of the 27th Fighter-
Escort Wing flew 180 F-84E aircraft from Bergstrom AFB to
air bases in Germany by using the North Atlantic Route.
These were the largest mass deployments of fighter aircraft
to that time.

Fursten-
feldbruck

U.K.

Iceland

Keflavik

Green-
land

Narsarssuak

Goose

McGuire

Bergstrom

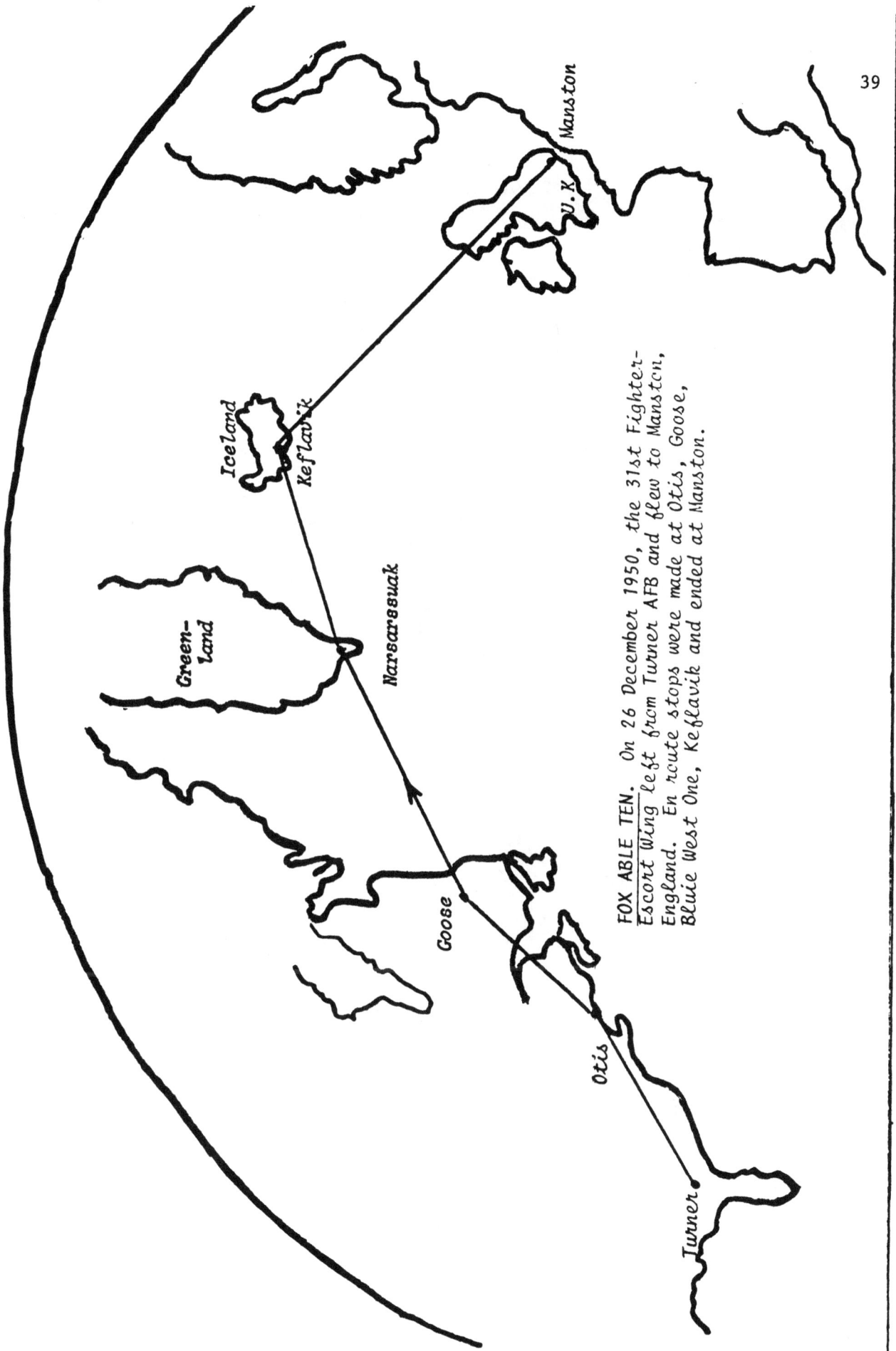

FOX ABLE TEN. On 26 December 1950, the 31st Fighter-Escort Wing left from Turner AFB and flew to Manston, England. En route stops were made at Otis, Goose, Bluie West One, Keflavik and ended at Manston.

MACKAY TROPHY

The MacKay Trophy is presented annually by the
Chief of Staff, USAF, to the Air Force person,
persons, or organization accomplishing the most
meritorious flight of the preceding calendar
year. The winners' names for each year are en-
graved on the trophy, which remains in the
custody of the Chief of Staff. The award was
temporarily suspended in 1916-1917 and during
World War II, but was reinstated 4 September
1946.

The MacKay Trophy was awarded to two SAC fighter units.

In 1950, it was awarded to the 27th Fighter
Escort Wing for Fox Able Three.

In 1953, it was awarded to the 40th Air
Division for Operation Longstride.

replacement unit signed for and assumed accountability for them. By 27 July, the personnel of the 31st FEW had departed for the home base.

In July 1951, the 12th FEW relieved the 31st FEW in England. The newly-assigned wing used the aircraft that the 31st FEW had signed over. For the next five months, the 12th FEW conducted training operations in the British Isles and on the continent. At the time of return to the United States, the 12th FEW signed the aircraft over to the 123rd Fighter-Bomber Wing, and the personnel of the 12 FEW returned to Bergstorm on 22 December 1951.

The return of the 12th FEW ended SAC's fighter overseas deployments to the United Kingdom for 1951. There were no deployments to European bases in 1952 and none until Operation Longstride in August 1953.

Rapid reaction was one of the hallmarks of SAC. Deployment and redeployment of fighters to overseas bases had been conducted for this purpose. Air refueling of a large number of fighters had been accomplished over the Pacific in 1952 (see below) which was significant in itself, but they also served to prepare for direct flights, nonstop across the Atlantic, from the United States to bases in Europe and North Africa. In the summer of 1953, SAC deployed fighters nonstop across the Atlantic in Operation Longstride.

Operation Longstride was the nonstop Atlantic crossing by the 31st SFW and the 508th SFW, both stationed at Turner AFB and assigned to the 40th Air Division. The operation was divided into two parts: one used the Central Atlantic route to Nouasseur AB, Morocco, and the other used the Northern Atlantic route to England. Both were refueled by several tanker units. Coca Alfa (Central Atlantic) One was the mission of the 31st SFW which used the Central Atlantic route. Nectar Alfa (North Atlantic) One was the mission of the 508th SFW and took the Northern Atlantic route (see map on following page). They both began on 20 August 1953.

Coca Alfa One began when nine F-84G from the 31st SFW took off from Turner AFB. One aircraft was a spare and it turned back at the coast while the eight remaining continued the flight. Two KC-97s from the 305th ARS(M) served as weather reconnaissance aircraft and ten others accomplished the refueling. The first refueling occurred near Bermuda and five KC-97s transferred the fuel. The second occurred over Ocean Vessel Y-E (located halfway between Bermuda and the Azores) from the second five tankers of the 305th ARS(M). Over the Azores, the third refueling was provided by five tankers from the 26th ARS(M). The eight F-84Gs landed at Nouasseur AB, Morocco with total elapsed time of ten hours and 20 minutes.

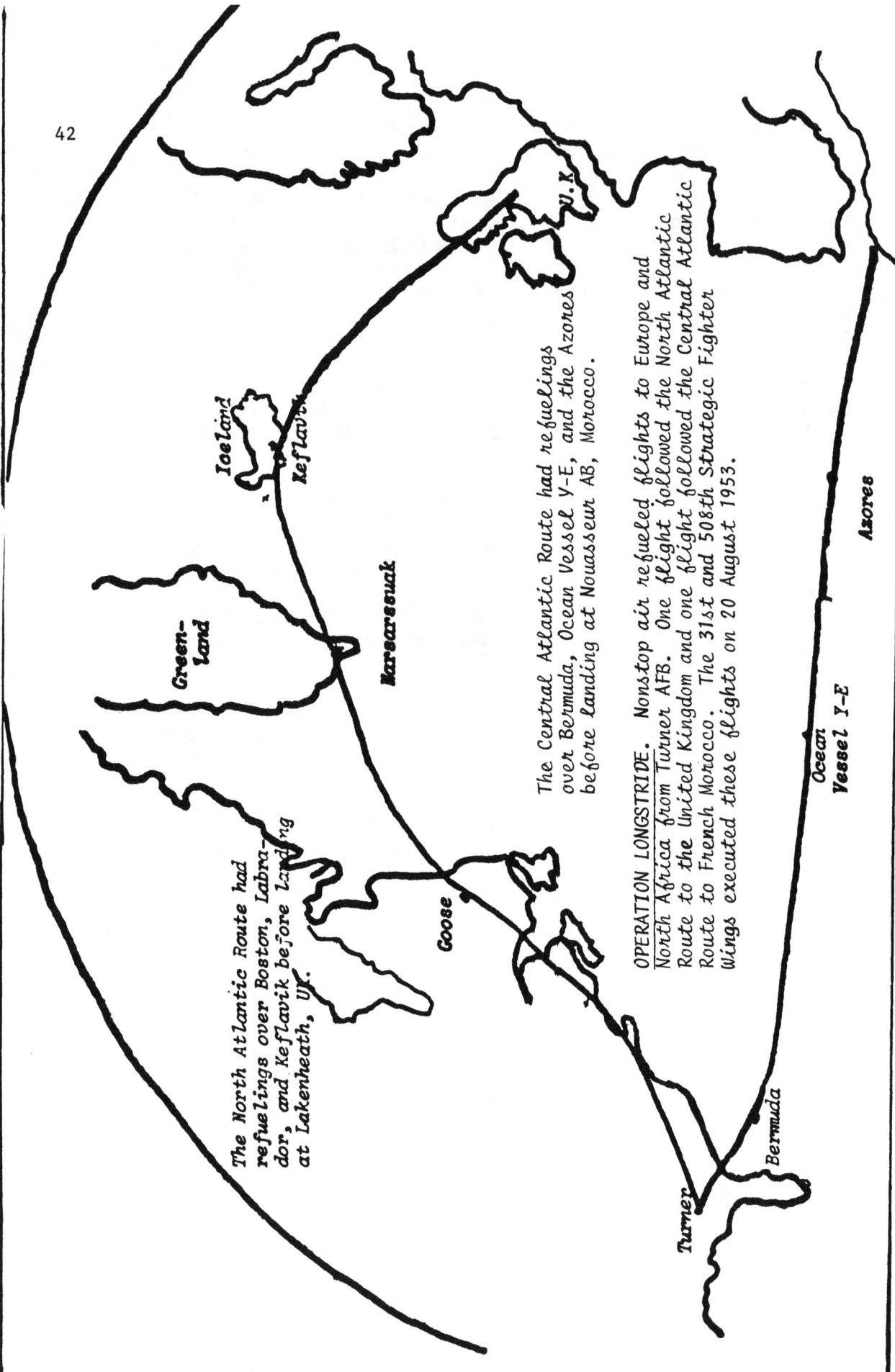

The North Atlantic Route had refuelings over Boston, Labrador, and Keflavik before landing at Lakenheath, UK.

The Central Atlantic Route had refuelings over Bermuda, Ocean Vessel Y-E, and the Azores before landing at Nouasseur AB, Morocco.

OPERATION LONGSTRIDE. Nonstop air refueled flights to Europe and North Africa from Turner AFB. One flight followed the North Atlantic Route to the United Kingdom and one flight followed the Central Atlantic Route to French Morocco. The 31st and 508th Strategic Fighter Wings executed these flights on 20 August 1953.

U.K.

Iceland

Keflavik

Green-land

Narsarssuak

Goose

Turner

Bermuda

Ocean Vessel Y-E

Azores

Nectar Alfa One was larger and involved 20 F-84Gs of the 508th SFW. They launched on 20 August 1953 and the first air refueling was provided by five KB-29Ps from the 100th ARS(M) over Boston. Eight KC-97s from the 26th ARS(M) provided the second refueling about 100 miles east of Cape Harrison, Labrador. The remaining aircraft continued and met six KC-97 tankers from the 7th Air Division for the third air refueling. Two additional fighters were prevented from taking fuel and had to abort to Keflavik AB, Iceland. Seventeen F-84Gs landed at Lakenheath, England. The total elapsed time was 11 hours and 20 minutes.

While in Morocco and England, the two fighter units conducted normal training and operational exercises. The fighters in Morocco flew to Lakenheath on 22 August for maintenance prior to the return flight. Coca Alfa One began redeployment along the Northern Route on 31 August and completed the first leg to Keflavik in less than four hours. The eight aircraft resumed the flight the next day and were refueled by four KB-29P tankers from the 100th ARS(M) over Bluie West One. One aircraft was damaged but all continued on to Limestone AFB (Loring), Maine. The damaged aircraft was left there and the remaining seven fighters took off the next day for Turner AFB. One aircraft aborted to Grenier AFB, New Hampshire, but rejoined the flight and landed at Turner AFB. The total distance flown by Coca Alfa One was 10,429 miles.

Redeployment of Nectar Alfa One started from Lakenheath on 9 September 1953, but due to high winds, the fighters landed at Prestwick, Scotland. The next leg was to Keflavik, Iceland, accomplished on 10 September where major items of maintenance were performed. The entire detachment left the next day for Goose Bay AB, Labrador, overflying Bluie West One. On 12 September 1953, all 20 F-84Gs landed at Turner AFB, completing Operation Longstride.

These two nonstop mass flights which were accomplished through air refueling were rated outstanding. Both the 31st SFW and the 508th SFW were assigned to the 40th Air Division. Headquarters USAF awarded the MacKay Trophy for 1953 to the 40th Air Division for Operation Longstride.

Rotations to Europe did not resume until May 1955 when the 27th SFW deployed from Bergstrom AFB. This rotation brought the F-84F to Europe and the Sturgate RAF Station for the first time. The wing used the Northern Atlantic route because, by 1955, air rescue facilities had become more elaborate and Bluie West One was a handy emergency landing field. Seventy-five F-84Fs in six flights (five of 12 aircraft and one of 15) flew in two stages. The first stage consisted of the flight from Bergstrom AFB to the first refueling point over Lockbourne AFB and then landing at Goose AB to a refueling track over Keflavik and then on to RAF Station Sturgate. The flight began on 2 May 1955 and by 9 May all 75 fighter aircraft were at Sturgate. There had been numerous aborts en route, but repairs were made quickly and the fighters managed to reach Sturgate in that short period of time.

The return flight was more significant. In the original draft of the plan, the 27th SFW proposed a mass nonstop flight to Bergstrom AFB for the whole wing. Flight safety provisions caused Headquarters SAC to disapprove, but the alternate proposal of 12 fighters flying all the way was approved. On 17 August 1955, the lead group of 12 F-84Fs took off from Sturgate. The nonstop element was refueled over Keflavik, again over Goose AB, and received the third off-load over Binghamton, New York. This element of the 27th SFW landed at Bergstrom AFB 10 hours and 43 minutes after take off (see map on following page). It was a record-breaking time.

The rest of the fighters staged through Keflavik to Goose AB and then to Bergstrom AFB. During the deployment and redeployment, only one aircraft was lost en route. The pilot had to abandon the aircraft over Texas when the engine failed. There were other losses incurred in the training program while the wing was on training flights in England.

The original program had called for the 506th SFW to replace the 27th SFW in the United Kingdom. Problems connected with aircraft delivery and engines prevented the 506th from taking part in the rotation. Instead, the 31st SFW of Turner AFB was substituted. Runway deterioration and repairs at Sturgate and Keflavik combined with slippages in the fighter delivery program caused SAC to cancel the rotation of the 31st SFW in August 1955. The cancellation proved to be the end of SAC fighter rotations to Europe and the United Kingdom (see Table 3). Rotations of SAC fighters to the Far East were different stories for no other reason than the vast distances involved.

SAC Fighter Deployments to Europe								Table 3
Unit	1948	1949	1950	1951	1952	1953	1954	1955	1956
12th				Jul-Dec					
27th			Sep-Oct FA-3					May-Aug F-84F	
31st			Dec-Jul FA-10			Longstride Aug		Aug(Canx)	
56th	Jul FA-1								
508th						Long- stride Aug	Oct		

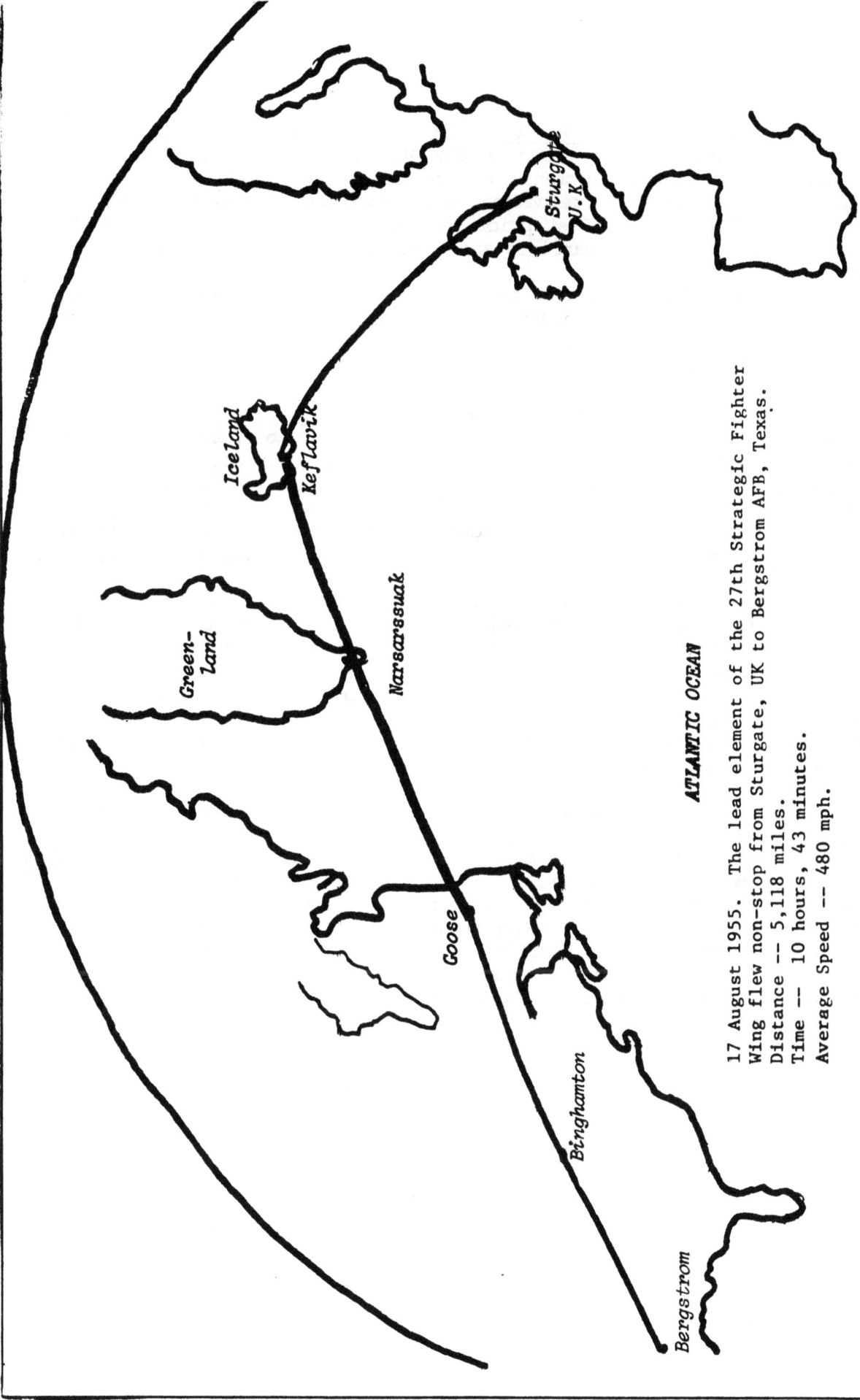

ATLANTIC OCEAN

17 August 1955. The lead element of the 27th Strategic Fighter
Wing flew non-stop from Sturgate, UK to Bergstrom AFB, Texas.
Distance -- 5,118 miles.
Time -- 10 hours, 43 minutes.
Average Speed -- 480 mph.

Ocean Crossings -- Pacific. Distances between land masses in the Pacific Ocean dwarfed those in the Atlantic. Hence, consideration of airborne fighter deployments had to be delayed until longer-range fighter aircraft and air refueling were developed. When SAC fighters were required in the Far East prior to these developments, the aircraft were loaded on U.S. Navy carriers and floated across the Pacific Ocean.

The 27th FEW exercised this naval support in November 1950. After the 27th's crews returned to Bergstrom from the F-84E ferry missions of Fox Able Three, preparations were made for TDY rotation to England. In the midst of these, the wing was ordered to Korea. Seventy-five aircraft were placed on board escort carriers at San Diego Naval Air Station on 11 November 1950. The USS Bairoka and the USS Bataan departed from San Diego on 14 and 16 November and arrived at Yokasuka, Japan, on 30 November 1950. The third carrier, the USS Cape Esperence, departed San Diego on 27 November and arrived in Japan on 13 December. First combat sortie was flown by the wing on 6 December 1950. After several months of combat operations, the wing returned to the United States in stages[*] without aircraft and equipment.

From 4 to 16 July 1952, the 31st Fighter-Escort Wing executed Fox Peter One, a pioneering flight that was the first mass in-flight fighter refueling mission to take place over any ocean (see map on following page). The wing flew from Turner AFB to Japan for a 90-day TDY to the Far East Air Forces. The first and second legs were from Turner to Travis to Hickam with one refueling on each leg. The remainder of the trip consisted of island-hopping flights from Hickam to Wake to Eniwetok to Guam to Iwo Jima and Japan.

Fox Peter One was unprecedented. It was arranged on short notice and required ingenious planning. For example, since no mass flight at wing strength employing air refueling had been done before, the first leg from Turner to Travis was used as a test profile mission. The difficulties encountered in the first air refueling over Texas were analyzed and corrected before the fighters and tankers took off for the second refueling over the Pacific. Prudently, precautionary provisions for air-sea rescue and weather scouting were arranged. Fortunately, no troubles developed and no additional refuelings were necessary for the remainder of the trip.

---

[*] All aircraft assigned to the 12th FEW were transferred to the 27th FEW on 12 July 1951.

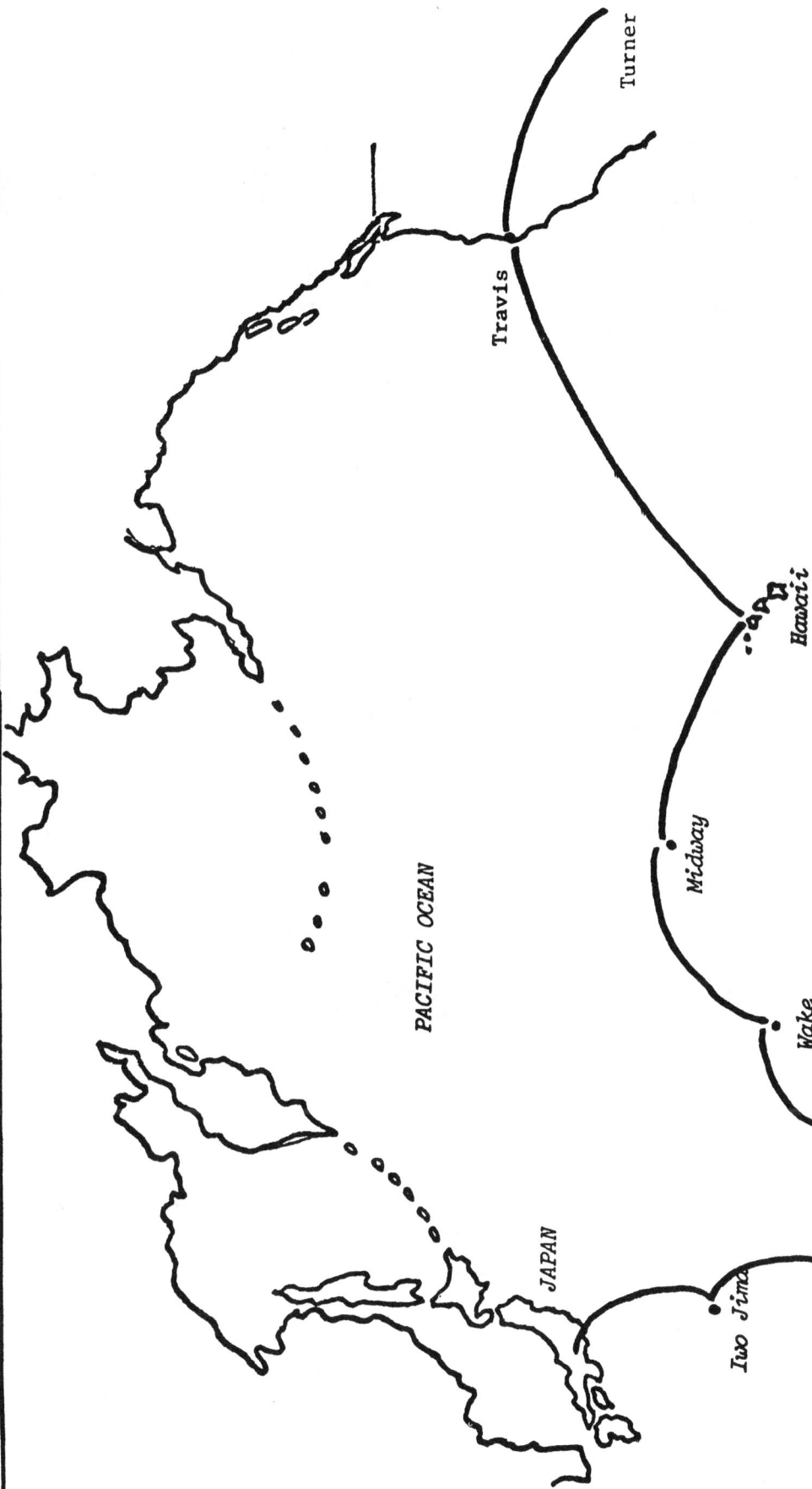

FOX PETER ONE. 31st Fighter-Escort Wing flew from Turner AFB, Georgia, to Japan. It was the first jet fighter wing to fly nonstop from the U.S. to Hawaii. From Hickam, the fighters island-hopped to Midway, to Wake, to Eniwetok, to Guam, to Iwo Jima, to Japan, a total of 10,670 miles. The 31st FEW was the first organization to receive the Air Force Outstanding Unit Award for this flight of F-84 aircraft.

Turner

Travis

Hawaii

Midway

Wake

Eniwetok

Guam

Iwo Jima

JAPAN

PACIFIC OCEAN

47

48

Development of mass mid-air refueling tactics and the experience gained from Fox Peter One demonstrated the feasibility and mobility of movement of large numbers of fighters by air refueling. General C. E. LeMay commented:

I desire to commend the 31st Fighter-Escort Wing for its unprecedented achievement in successfully completing the movement of fifty-eight F-84G aircraft from Turner Air Force Base, Albany, Georgia, to Japan. This operation is the first long-range over-water mass jet flight in Air Force history utilizing in-flight refueling techniques and has materialized a capability heretofore considered improbable. Operation Fox Peter One is another "first" reflecting great credit upon the United States Air Force as well as the Strategic Air Command.

General LeMay also praised the 307th Air Refueling Squadron, Medium, for its support of the mission in the following manner:

The 307th Air Refueling Squadron was particularly selected for the most critical point of the entire flight, Ocean Station "Uncle," because of the outstanding record it had compiled during its routine training. It was known that those fighter aircraft requiring refueling at "Uncle" would have to be success fully refueled or be lost at sea. The 307th Air Refueling Squadron performed its mission faultlessly during this operation, successfully completing each refueling contact requested by the fighter aircraft.

General Nathan B. Twining, Air Force Vice Chief of Staff, expressed similar sentiments:

I have been very impressed with the recent accomplishment of the 31st FEW on their flight to Japan. I believe they did an exceptional job and especially in view of their short notice and the mechanical difficulties they experienced on the way. The extra range of the F-84G with single point refueling provides the aircraft with a real capability in addition to its special mission possibilities.

Because of the success of the mission, the 31st Strategic Fighter Wing received the Air Force Outstanding Unit Award on 23 February 1954.

Valuable conclusions were reached. With air refuelings, F-84 flights over water to maximum range were practicable. With prestocked jet fuel at all refueling stops, jet fighters could be deployed to the Far East under their own power. The final report of Fox Peter One recommended a route refinement: that the flights from Midway go direct either to Iwo Jima or to Japan with one air refueling and shorten the distance.

Fox Peter Two was the deployment of the 27th FEW to replace the 31st FEW in Japan in October 1952 (see map on following page). In Fox Peter Two, the 75 F-84G fighters of the 27th FEW followed the recommendation. They left Bergstrom and followed the same procedures as the 31st FEW to Travis, Hickam, and Midway. From Midway, the fighters flew direct to Misawa AB, Japan, accomplishing one air refueling on the way. The last leg of the flight was a nonstop flight of 2,575 miles, the longest over-water refueling flight in single-engine jet fighter history to that time.

These two flights were momentous. After Fox Peter Two, the F-84G aircraft remained in Japan and rotational fighter units used them when TDY. The rotations were as follows:

October 1952	27th FEW replaced the 31st FEW
February 1953	508th SFW replaced the 27th SFW
May 1953	12th SFW replaced the 508th SFW
August 1953	506th SFW replaced the 12th SFW
November 1953	31st SFW replaced the 506th SFW
February 1954	508th SFW replaced the 31st SFW
May 1954	12th SFW replaced the 508th SFW
August 1954	407th SFW replaced the 12th SFW

SAC had begun seeking relief from these rotations shortly after the Korean truce talks had begun.

Analysis of Overseas Rotations. SAC requested relief from fighter wing rotation to support FEAF. The problem was centered in the divergence between the SAC fighter mission and the tasks assigned to the fighter wing TDY in Japan. While in Japan, the SAC fighters performed a Japan Air Defense Force (JADF) alert mission which did not contribute to either the escort mission or later to the strategic mission. Besides, although the TDY requirement was only for 90 days, SAC's fighter units had to abandon the full pursuit of their training requirements for a total period of five months. While TDY to Japan, little training was accomplished that advanced the primary mission of the SAC fighter wings.

In 1952, Headquarters SAC had requested that USAF obtain fighter wings for rotation from other sources if at all practicable. General Thomas D. White, Air Force Vice Chief of Staff, told General LeMay that the demands on SAC since the Korean War were appreciated. Nevertheless, fighter augmentation was necessary in FEAF and SAC possessed the only available resources. Hence, SAC would continue the rotation program.

This complicated issue was further compounded by the aircraft conversion program which caused the fighter wings to reequip with newer models. Besides, the mission change for the development of atomic capability in the SAC fighter wings established further demands on the time

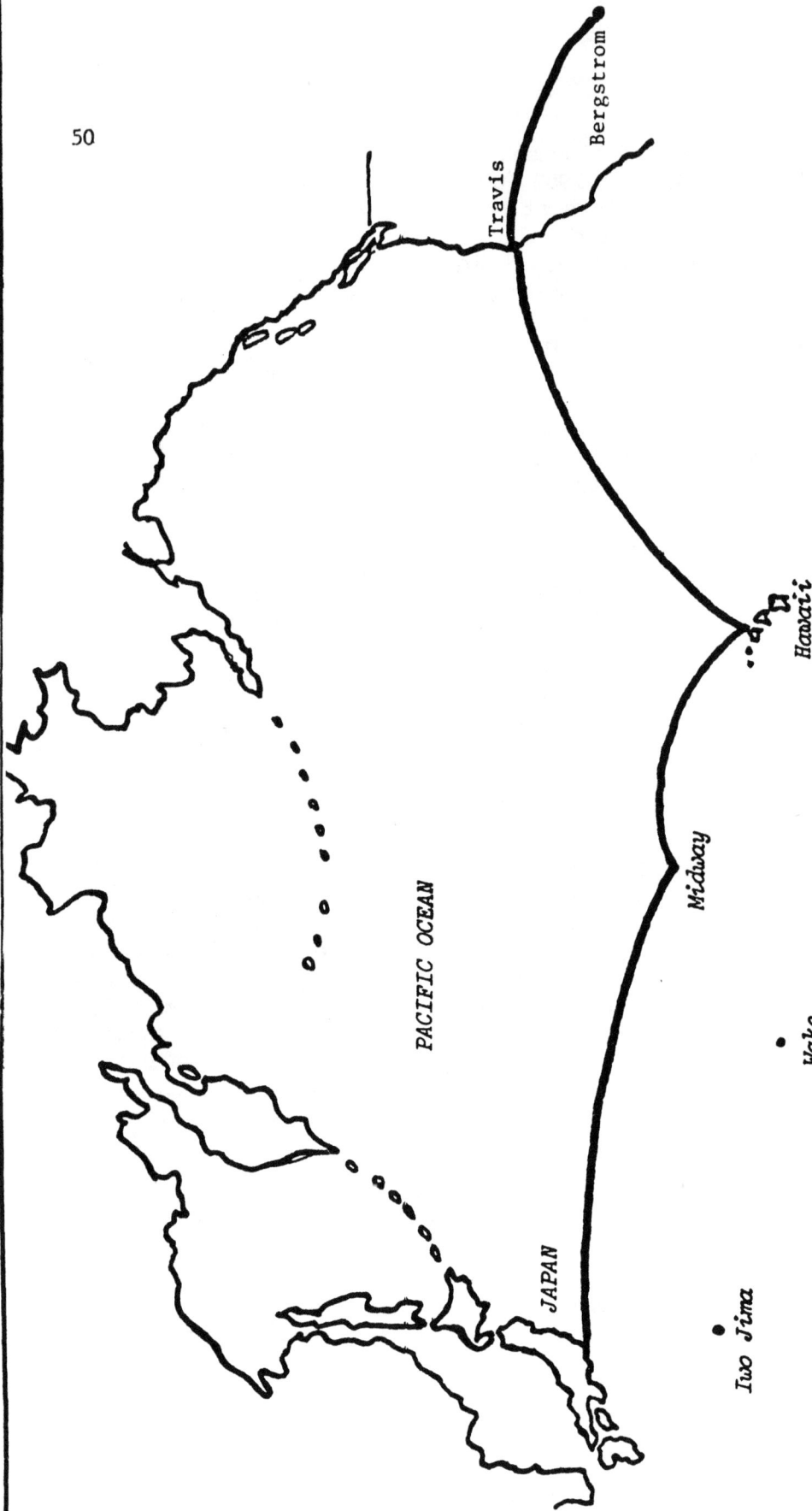

50

FOX PETER TWO. The 27th Fighter-Escort Wing flew from Bergstrom AFB, Texas, to Travis AFB, California, on 3 October 1952. With one refueling, the wing flew to Hickam AFB, Hawaii, and then to Midway. From Midway, the wing flew to Japan with one refueling. This last leg from Midway to Misawa was the longest overwater refueling flight in single-engine jet fighter history to that time, 2,575 miles. Total distance, 7,800 miles.

and proficiency of the crews. Performing an air defense mission in Japan did not contribute to or coincide with the SAC primary fighter mission.

Headquarters SAC pressed for relief through 1953 and justified its request most firmly on 8 January 1954, as follows:

1. All SFWs have completed a TDY tour to FEAF since 4 July 1952.

2. All SFWs are presently attaining a special weapons capability. Rotation of any wing to FEAF will interrupt their training as SAC's F-84s in FEAF do not have LABS equipment installed and are not equipped for celestial navigation.

3. Four fighter wings within the ZI have an assigned EWP mission . . . Rotation of crews who have assigned targets in the EWP necessitates the reassignment of EWP targets causing an increased security risk. . . .

4. Continuing SFW rotations to FEAF will curtail the maneuver training of SFWs in the United Kingdom and North Africa.

5. The Air Defense role of SFWs on FEAF rotation is not the primary mission of the SFWs.

6. Informal comments from all SFW commanders indicate that the F-84G aircraft in its geographical location in Japan in conjunction with early warning is unsuitable for performing the assigned mission.

Headquarters SAC concluded the request with remarks and recommendations as follows:

1. Continued rotation of SAC fighter wings . . . will result in unacceptable deterioration of the SAC fighter force.

2. If a . . . requirement exists, it would be less costly, both in money and combat capability, to permanently assign a fighter unit to FEAF.

3. Rotation and maneuvers of SAC fighter wings would be restricted to testing of unit mobility plans and deployment through overseas bases proposed for use in support of EWP.

During the rotation of the 31st SFW to Japan in 1953 and 1954, Colonel Schilling noted that lost time and lack of available low altitude bombing system (LABS) equipment caused the degraded training. The 508th SFW succeeded Colonel Schilling's 31st SFW in Japan in February 1954. The commander of the 508th pointed out the loss in combat crew and primary mission training as a result of the rotation. He noted that combat crew training practically ceased on 15 January 1954 to prepare for departure. Limited training began in Japan on 15 February 1954, but it was halted once again on 1 May 1954 to permit preparations for the return home. As a result, of the 5,295 hours flown under the Japan Air Defense Force commitment only 2,000 hours were flown in accomplishing SAC proficiency requirements. The air defense commitment was a limiting factor. LABS equipment was not available. Serious training did not begin back at the home base until 1 June 1954.

On many occasions, the fighter units would return from overseas deployment without their aircraft. In these instances, the unit would have to be reequipped either with the same models or more advanced ones. As a consequence, the period devoted to build up and attaining combat readiness was lost from normal proficiency training. The 508th SFW commander also pointed out that if the wing had kept its own aircraft and had flown them to the rotation TDY duty station, at least 9,000 hours flying time could have been accomplished during the four and one-half month period. The irony of it all was that a FEAF organization, the 49th Fighter-Bomber Wing, did not stand JADF alert and instead practiced special weapons delivery. On this basis, he recommended:

1. No SAC fighter wings should be rotated to Japan unless they are able to take their own equipment with them so as to be able to train for their primary mission. Also, if SAC fighter wings rotate to Japan, the air defense of those islands should be divided on a more equitable basis between the SAC unit and the unit permanently assigned there. This would allow the aircrews to concentrate on combat crew training and training for its primary mission.

2. The continuous transfer of aircraft by one wing to another should cease. A fighter wing retaining its own aircraft would insure against a loss of combat crew training flying time.

The two years of requests for relief by Headquarters SAC was honored in late 1954. The last unit assigned TDY to Japan was the 407th SFW which spent 120 days there from August through November 1954 (see Table 4).

On occasion, SAC's fighters would deploy overseas for special missions. For example, the 11th Bombardment Wing's B-36 dropped an atomic bomb in the Atomic Energy Commission's test program on 16 November 1952. This test program was identified as Operation Ivy and involved 32 crews and 16 F-84Gs of the 12 Fighter-Escort Wing and two KB-29Ps of the 307th Air Refueling Squadron, Medium. Special modifications to the aircraft equipped them to collect samples of atomic clouds, but it also precluded their usefulness to the War Plan. Hence, one squadron of the 12th FEW was relieved of its responsibilities in this category because of its participation in the project. The crews engaged in special training in long-range navigation, cruise control, rendezvous, and

SAC FIGHTER FAR EAST AIR FORCES DEPLOYMENTS

Table 4

Unit	1950	1951	1952	1953	1954
12th			(Ivy)--Mar-Dec	May-Aug	May-Aug
27th	Nov-----Jul		(Fox Peter Two)	Oct--Feb	
31st			(Fox Peter One) Jul-Oct	Nov----Feb	
407th					Aug-Nov
506th				Aug-Nov	
508th				Feb-May	Feb-May

inflight refueling. The crews flew these aircraft into the atomic cloud to collect samples and to measure the effects of heat and blast on tactical aircraft. The aircraft and personnel of the detachment moved from Bergstrom AFB to Kwajalein Atoll in early October 1952. After the bomb drop in mid-November, the F-84s were sent back to the United States on a U.S. Navy escort carrier, USS Rendova, and arrived back at Bergstrom on 22 November 1952.

Any examination of rotations assignments had to take into consideration the use of the tankers. Each time a tanker unit rotated or was used in support of an overseas deployment, it meant a loss of training to the parent bombardment wing. This problem was more critical during the years when the expansion program was underway. More wings were requiring training, but not all wings were supported by an air refueling squadron.

SAC Fighters in Korea

The 27th FEW had completed the ferrying of 180 F-84E aircraft to Europe (Fox Able Three) in October 1950. The wing was also scheduled for TDY rotation to England but this was canceled on 9 November 1950 and the 27th was ordered to Korea. Two days later, 66 F-84Es left Bergstrom on the first leg to North Island NAS, San Diego, California. Fourteen aircraft arrived the next day and 75 F-84Es were loaded on USN escort

carriers for shipment to Japan. Although the voyage was free from incidents, corrosion from salt water and from ships' exhaust had done a lot
of damage and caused a week of maintenance.

Two of the aircraft carriers arrived at Yokasuka, Japan, on 30
November and the third arrived on 13 December 1950. The 27th FEW flew
the first operational sortie on an armed reconnaissance mission on 6
December 1950. By the end of the month, the wing had flown 927 effective sorties. Between 6 December 1950 and 15 July 1951 when the 27th
FEW was relieved by the 136th Fighter-Bomber Wing, the SAC F-84Es flew
13,110 effective sorties with only 11 aircraft lost to enemy action.

The type of sorties ran the full range of fighter capabilties.
They included close support of United Nations ground forces. The 27th
Wing Commander stated after several months of close support that the
F-84E was the best ground support jet aircraft in Korea. Other
missions included armed reconnaissance, combat air patrol, interdiction,
and flak suppression. SAC's fighters also flew escort sorties for
B-29s. In this mission, the F-84Es engaged in air-to-air combat with
MIG-15s, destroying the first one on 21 January 1951. The major
problem with escort flying occurred with F-86 aircraft. The F-84 crews
noted that the silhouette profile of the F-86 and the MIG-15 were
strongly similar. Even though the crews were thoroughly briefed on the
unique distinctive features of the F-86, there was some hesitation to
fire when a MIG was locked in the sights. Such hesitation permitted
some MIGs to escape.

The mission of the 27th FEW in Korea began to taper off on 1
June 1951 when the 522nd Fighter Escort Squadron was relieved from combat responsibilities. On 21 May 1951, the 182nd Fighter-Bomber Squadron
was assigned to Korea and attached to the 27th Fighter-Escort Group. It
became fully operational on 1 June when the 522nd was relieved and flew
sorties with the other two squadrons of the 27th FEW, the 523rd and
524th FES, during the month of June 1951. By the end of June, the 154th
FES relieved the 523rd FES which, along with the 27th FEG, were relieved
from combat responsibilities. The 27th FEW closed its headquarters in
Japan on 15 July and opened them at Bergstrom AFB the next day. The one
remaining squadron, the 524th continued to fly sorties during the month
of July and accumulated 337 effective sorties and 923 hours of combat
flying time. All aircraft and equipment of the 27th FEW were transferred to the 136th FBW which retained them in Korea. SAC's 27th FEG
was awarded the Distinguished Unit Citation for its combat record in
Korea.

Fighter Competition

Although bombing competitions had become an annual affair,
there was only one fighter competition ever held. From 25 October 1956
to 14 November 1956, SAC's strategic fighter wings competed against each
other. The basis was a Unit Simulated Combat Mission (USCM) that was

held at SAC Headquarters, Offutt AFB, Nebraska. Only one wing at a time occupied the base and each wing sent 36 aircraft and crews. The course was the same for all and each wing's participants were divided into 18 elements of two aircraft each. Each element (leader and wingman) flew separately at intervals of ten minutes. The course started at Offutt and the first leg of the flight was to Bemidji Airfield, Minnesota. This leg was flown at 500 feet in a controlled period of time. At Bemidji, the aircraft turned and climbed to 35,000 feet and headed toward Grand Island, Nebraska. Near Grand Island they descended to 7,000 feet and refueled from KB-29P tankers. After refueling, the elements headed for Camp Phillips, Kansas, and its bombing range. Until they approached the target, the altitude was 15,000 feet. On the bomb run, the lead aircraft descended to 500 feet for the bomb run. The wingman followed but at a higher altitude. After these two made a rendezvous, they returned to Offutt, flying at 22,000 feet. The three and one-half hour mission was flown nonstop in standard F-84Fs. All through the flight they were tracked by ground radar and spotters and were subject to interception by F-89s.

Scoring was based on navigation, bombing, and maintenance. The final wing scores were:

Final Wing Scores

Wing	Navigation	Bombing	Maintenance	Briefing	Total
506th	12,250	28,813	12,500	1,000	54,563
31st	13,169	24,550	13,500	1,000	52,219
12th	11,715	20,138	12,000	1,000	44,853
27th	13,049	16,954	13,500	1,000	44,503
407th	12,146	12,237	12,500	1,000	37,883

These performance ratings were satisfactory. The competition demonstrated that the SAC fighter force could penetrate and navigate to an assigned target and deliver a weapon with required accuracy. The maintenance and reliability were outstanding. Of the 180 aircraft in the competition, only nine aborted. The target was exceptionally difficult and the weather was bad, yet the bombing was considered highly satisfactory. All the fighters were gone from SAC in July 1957 and, thus, the 1956 Fighter Competition was the only one ever held.

Changes in Tactics with Atomic Capability

Tactics employed by fighter crews with a mission of bomber escort were vastly different from those for delivery of atomic weapons. When the primary mission was expanded to include atomic delivery, the conversion compelled the wings to achieve and maintain operational capability with these weapons. Aircraft had to be modified, crews had to be trained in the new bombing techniques, and the crews had to maintain proficiency. Although the concept was adopted in December 1952, and the designation of the wings changed in January 1953, actual training in the various techniques did not begin until January 1954. The cause for the lapse in time was the bombing systems had not arrived on the bases until September 1953. Regardless, testing had begun in late 1952.

The standard A-4 and A-7 bomb sights on the F-84G aircraft in late 1952 were inadequate for atomic bomb delivery on a low-level penetration route. Air Research and Development Command (ARDC) had available a Low Altitude Bombing System (LABS) which was determined to be a product of the best technology of the period. Since it was the best available for fighter low altitude atomic delivery, Headquarters USAF established a requirement to install it on all fighters with an atomic mission. It was the best equipment available, but it, too, was limited although these limitations were considered transient. To test the LABS equipment with two different techniques, SAC initiated Project Kick-Off in November 1952.

The two different techniques were identified as the Pathfinder Delivery and the Vertical Angle Release. The 31st FEW tested the Pathfinder which was also used by other commands with a fighter atomic mission. It was also referred to as the LABS method. The 12th FEW tested the Vertical Angle Release (VAR) method which was developed solely by SAC. Both tests employed the LABS equipment.

The 31st FEW concentrated on the LABS Pathfinder Delivery method. In the case, the pilot used the radar gun-sight and an automatic pull-up control system. The use of the pull-up system in conjunction with the aircraft's autopilot practically eliminated all human reaction time errors. The shortcoming was that an exact initial point (IP) had to be known. Delivery techniques during the tests included flying at 1,000 feet altitude, approaching the target at 500 miles per hour, a 45° angle of release, and 18,600 feet as the basic range from the target to the start of the pull-up. At the conclusion of this part of the test in June 1953, the circular error was averaged at 1,500 feet (see illustration on following page).

The 12th FEW tested the VAR technique. This employed the same speed and altitude criteria, but the difference was that the pilot executed a loop, so positioned that while in the vertical part of the loop, the aircraft would be positioned directly over the target. At this point, the LABS computer released the bomb automatically and the pilot continued with an Immelman turn while completing the loop. There were two disadvantages with the VAR. One was that the start of the loop had to be exact and any error was carried over into the impact area and a large azimuth error could be expected. The second disadvantage was that while executing the Immelman directly over the target, the aircraft was exceedingly vulnerable to anti-aircraft artillery (AAA) fire for about 30 seconds. Nevertheless, the test had proved it feasible (see illustration on second following page).

VERTICAL CLIMB RELEASE

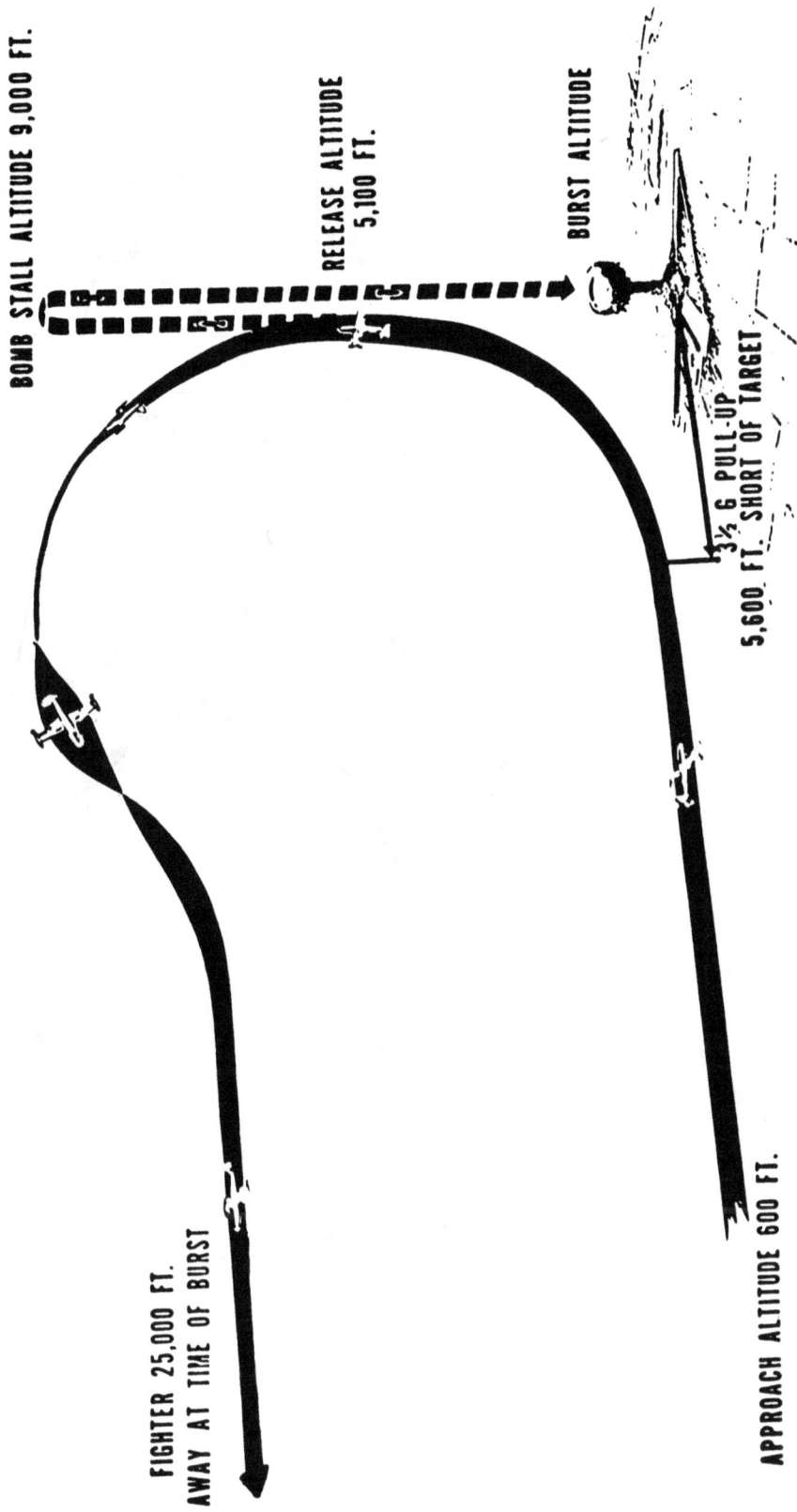

BOMB STALL ALTITUDE 9,000 FT.

RELEASE ALTITUDE 5,100 FT.

BURST ALTITUDE

3½ G PULL-UP

5,600 FT. SHORT OF TARGET

FIGHTER 25,000 FT. AWAY AT TIME OF BURST

APPROACH ALTITUDE 600 FT.

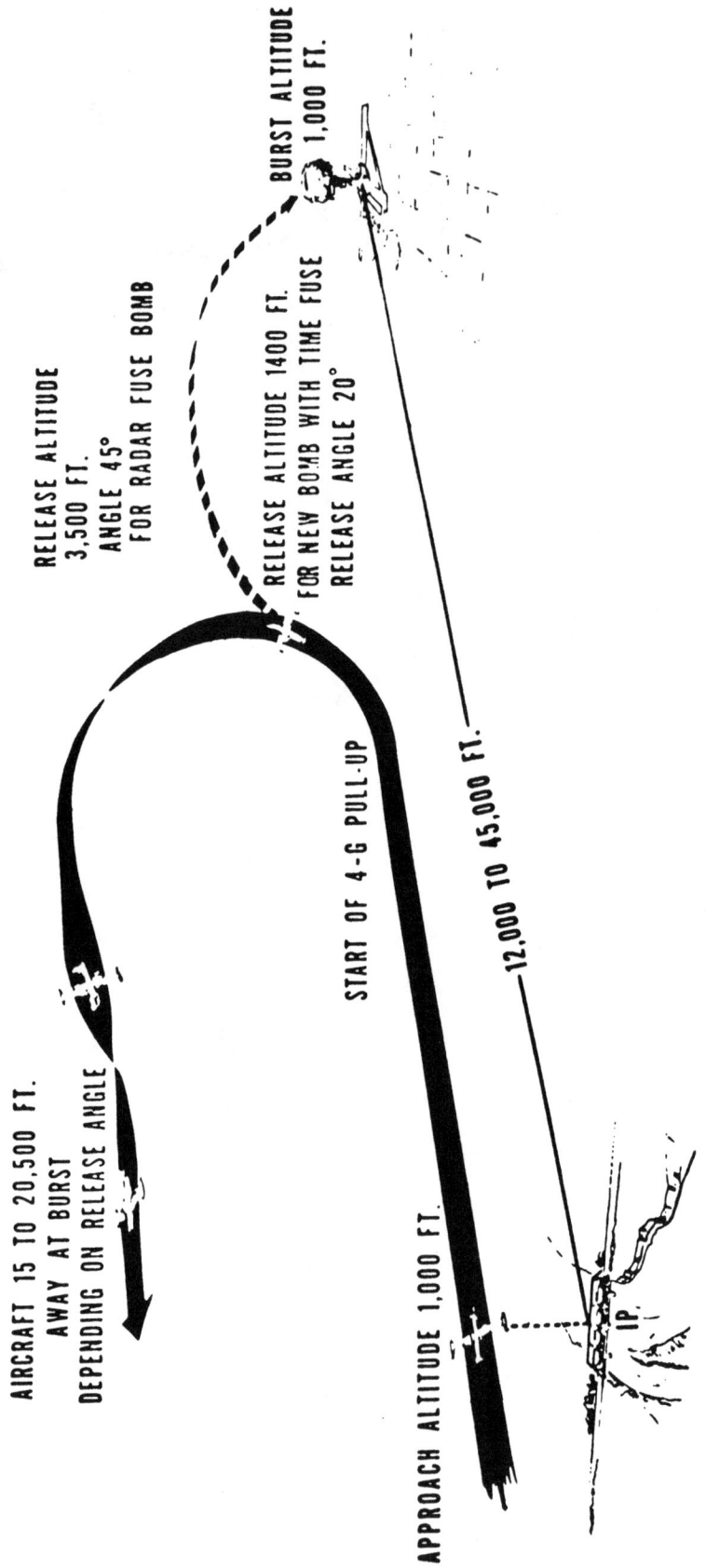

58

LABS RELEASE

RELEASE ALTITUDE
3,500 FT.
ANGLE 45°
FOR RADAR FUSE BOMB

BURST ALTITUDE
1,000 FT.

RELEASE ALTITUDE 1400 FT.
FOR NEW BOMB WITH TIME FUSE
RELEASE ANGLE 20°

AIRCRAFT 15 TO 20,500 FT.
AWAY AT BURST
DEPENDING ON RELEASE ANGLE

START OF 4-G PULL-UP

12,000 TO 45,000 FT.

APPROACH ALTITUDE 1,000 FT.

IP

Further testing of the VAR delivery technique occurred in September and October 1953. It showed that the VAR delivery technique as developed by SAC provided a direct, simple, and flexible method of delivering atomic bombs. On this basis, SAC adopted the Vertical Angle Release (VAR) as the primary tactic and the LABS as the secondary tactic.

There was also a third technique. In this procedure, the aircraft approached the target at 8,000 feet, dove to 7,000 feet, and released the bomb on a tossed trajectory. Once released, the pilot executed a loop and departed. This was not considered practicable because of the long exposure to ground fire at a vulnerable altitude.

Although the aircraft were modified, aircrews trained, weapons specialists assigned, and tactics developed, the SAC fighter wings never possessed nuclear weapons.

60

Summary

The SAC fighter aircraft program was part of the mission and organization of the command from 1 May 1946 to 1 July 1957. The period of the first four years was one in which the course followed was erratic and uncertain in the number of units assigned and in the type of aircraft used. It was succeeded by the remaining period which was characterized by stability and growth in the organizations devoted to the escort mission.

In these eleven years, SAC's fighter program extended overseas first by using U.S. Navy aircraft carriers, then by hopping from point-to-point, and later when air refueling became practicable, by flying direct to the overseas bases. Along with the expanded program was the expanded mission when the ability to deliver atomic bombs was added to the SAC fighters.

The thread running through the fighter program was SAC's requirement for a fighter that would meet the standards for an escort aircraft. None was ever obtained that fully met the standards, but the SAC crews performed their missions with aircraft that were unable to do the job perfectly.

In the last year of the program, SAC was in the process of transferring its fighter units to TAC. Headquarters SAC had requested a reduction of the fighter force earlier on the grounds that the funds could be better used in the bomber program. Bases were also needed for the rapidly expanding bomber force of B-47 and B-52 bombers, neither of which really needed escort fighters. In addition, the B-36 was slated for retirement. In early 1957, General Nathan F. Twining, Air Force Chief of Staff, spoke of the SAC fighter escorts: "These units existed primarily to assist the slower B-36s in reaching their targets and are eliminated in favor of higher priority forces."

Although SAC went out of the fighter business in 1957 for all intents and purposes, in 1958 it found itself assigned fighters again. On 1 July 1958, the 497th Fighter Interceptor Squadron, formerly a TAC unit, was assigned to SAC and arrived at Torrejon AB, Spain from Geiger Field, Washington on 5 July 1958. Another fighter squadron, the 431st moved from Wheelus, Tripoli, arriving at Zaragoza in September. Both squadrons were equipped with F-86Ds. Their mission was base defense. (History of SAC, June 1958 to July 1959, pg 223).

In April 1960, the 497th began conversion from F-86Ds to F-102As and had 26 F-102As on 30 June 1960. On the next day, both the 497th and 431st were transferred from Strategic Air Command to USAFE in order that all USAF fighter assets in Europe could be concentrated in one command. (Hist of 16th AF, July-Dec 1960).

APPENDIX I

Fighter Aircraft

Fighter aircraft were known by many suffixes: fighter-bomber, fighter-escort, and fighter-interceptor. They performed many different missions that included bombing, rocketry, ground and aerial gunnery, interception of penetrators, and escort of bomber and reconnaissance aircraft. These missions overlapped with only vague lines of separation. Basic to SAC's fighter problems was that no planes had been specifically designed for escort work. The escort fighters had been designed to fill multiple functions and thereby diluted the escort abilities. Consequently, the fighters assigned to the command for escort duties lacked the ability to fly long-range escort missions adequately. No airplanes were available to fly escort missions and engage enemy interceptors on equal or superior terms.

Piston-Engined Fighters

Eleven years before the termination of the fighter mission, Headquarters USAAF had recognized the limitations of the piston-engined fighters and predicted their demise by 1948. SAC retained the older piston-engined fighters until August 1949, and then they were reintroduced in March 1951 for eight months. In 1946, the only available escort fighter for SAC was the P-51H.

P/F-51H,* Mustang. There were three fighter groups equipped with P-51H aircraft, the first fighter assigned to SAC. The first active group was the 56th Fighter Group, stationed at Selfridge Field, Michigan, and activated on 1 May 1946 with aircraft arriving the next month. By October, the 56th had built up to its authorized UE of 75 aircraft. After one of the squadrons made a short trip to Alaska, the 56th began a conversion program on 23 April 1947 that changed the UE from P-51H aircraft to P-80A.

The second active P-51H fighter group was the 82nd, stationed at Grenier Army Air Base, New Hampshire. P-51Hs began arriving on the base in August 1947. Two years later, the 82nd Fighter Wing was relieved from assignment to SAC and assigned to the Continental Air Command.

---

* Designation of fighters was changed from "P" to "F" on 11 June 1948.

64

F-82 "Twin Mustangs" of the 27th Fighter Wing on the ramp at Kearney AFB, Nebraska in 1948. The F-82 served SAC as an escort fighter from 1947-1950.

SAC's first fighter was the P-51 Mustang, a single-engined fighter that gained fame during World War II. Three SAC groups were equipped with the P-51, later designed F-51.

33rd Fighter Group P-51s on the ramp at
Roswell Army Air Field, New Mexico, 1947

27th Fighter Escort Wing F-82

In 1947, SAC received its first jet aircraft, the P-80 "Shooting Star"

F-84G of SAC's 31st Fighter Escort Wing during a 1950 aerial refueling

The third active fighter group to be equipped with the P-51H aircraft was the 33rd Fighter Group, activated at Roswell Army Air Base on September 1947. Although aircraft began arriving the next month, the P-51 remained unit equipment for only a short time. By June 1948, the 33rd converted to jet-propelled fighters, the F-84B.

Thus, three fighter groups were equipped with P-51s. Only in the case of the 82nd Fighter Group did the aircraft remain as unit equipment for more than several months. The tenure of the P-51H in SAC lasted only two years in that unit with the longest continuity. By 22 August 1949, the P-51s were gone from SAC with one exception.

The exception occurred during the Korean War. In March and April 1951, four Air National Guard units were assigned to SAC. One of the wings possessed F-47D aircraft as its standard equipment, two possessed F-51D aircraft, and one possessed a combination of F-51D and F-84B/C aircraft. The inclusion of the four ANG fighter wings in SAC's fighter force was a temporary retrogression to piston-engined fighters. While these units were part of SAC, they contributed little to the escort abilities because their airplanes were not considered adequate as escort aircraft for long-range, high-speed bombardment aircraft. The only other piston-engined fighter assigned to SAC was the F-82.

P/F-82E, Twin Mustang. In its search for an adequate escort fighter, SAC turned to an aircraft which it considered an "interim" escort fighter, the P/F-82. This aircraft was considered to fit into the long-range operations of the command better than anything possessed to that time. The only unit equipped with the P/F-82 was the 27th Fighter Wing which was activated at Kearney AFB, Nebraska, on 15 August 1947. The first aircraft arrived on 23 January 1948 and the wing was rated combat ready by 31 December 1948. The 27th Fighter Wing and its aircraft moved to Bergstrom AFB, Texas, in May 1949. In December 1949, the 27th FEW began conversion to F-84Es. The F-82s were transferred to other commands on a staggered basis, beginning in June 1950. On 1 July 1950, there were 59 F-82s left in the 27th FEW. Thirty-two of these were transferred in July and the remaining 27 in August 1950. Other than the temporary retrogression of the four ANG fighter wings being assigned to SAC, the use of piston-engined fighters terminated with the last of the F-82s in the 27th FEW. SAC was then completely equipped with jet fighters.

Jet-Propulsion Fighters

When the 27th FEW dropped the last F-82 from its assets in August 1950, a four-year period of transition came to an end. In those four years, jet and conventional aircraft had existed on equal terms within the command. Nevertheless, the days of the conventional aircraft had been numbered when the jet engines and aircraft had been developed during the war years. The delivery of operational fighters equipped with jet engines began in 1945.

12th Fighter Escort Wing F-84s at Sola, Norway in 1951

Lockheed Aircraft Corporation delivered the first P-80A aircraft which was the first USAAF jet-propelled aircraft in December 1945. In June 1946, Brigadier General Charles F. Born, first commander of the Fifteenth Air Force, strongly recommended that the jet fighters be acquired for the 56th Fighter Group. In justification, General Born pointed out that any enemy fighters encountered in the future would undoubtedly be jets and to protect bombers from such attacks, escort fighters would have to be comparable. He recognized that the P-80A range limitations precluded it from becoming a suitable escort fighter, but he stressed the advantages in getting started with new tactics and new developments. Thus, new tactics evolved through experience would keep the forces ahead of any enemy. He said, "If this command has only the equipment and tactics of the past war to guide our training principles, it will remain stagnant and assume an unwarranted feeling of security." He felt the advantages in converting one very long range fighter group outweighed the disadvantages. He recommended that SAC have up-to-date fighters for escort purposes. Headquarters USAAF held the same views because next month it stated that the first-line aircraft would be the P-80, P-84, and P-86, replacing the P-47 and P-51.

P-80A, Shooting Star. In April 1947, two of SAC's fighter groups, the 4th and 56th, began receiving P-80A aircraft. This first USAAF jet fighter offered many possibilities, but during 1947 its tactical suitability was still in question. In fact, for the first six months, the 56th Fighter Group limited its operations to air shows and a few practice escort missions with B-29s. It wasn't until October 1947, that the 63rd Fighter Squadron of the 56th Fighter Group flew eight of its P-80As from Selfridge to Fort Worth AAF for a series of tests to determine the P-80A's combat potential. The test sorties determined clearly that the range capacity of the P-80 fighter was far less than desired for an escort fighter. Even with the addition of wing-tip tanks, its radius of escort cover extended only to 425 miles.

During 1948, one of the difficulties with the P-80 was resolved. Maintenance technical problems of jet operations and jet engines had been solved. As a consequence, the P-80A was considered tactically reliable by the end of the year which was a rapid progression compared to others that would follow it. However, the range limitations revealed in the October 1947 tests forecast its demise in SAC. On 1 December 1948, the two F-80 groups were relieved from assignment to SAC and assigned to the Continental Air Command for air defense purposes. Thus, the F-80 passed out of the SAC fighter force.

Two F-84Fs of the 27th Fighter Group stationed at Bergstrom AFB, Texas. This was a swept-wing version of the F-84.

F-86A, Sabrejet. SAC's possession of the F-86A which was exclusively a fighter-interceptor was a unique experience with the 1st Fighter Wing.* On 1 May 1949, SAC assumed command jurisdiction of March AFB, California, from Continental Air Command and inherited the 1st Fighter Wing along with the base. The 1st Fighter Wing was equipped with the F-86A and this aircraft had little long-range potential. Furthermore, the latent defects in the aircraft consumed an inordinate amount of maintenance effort on an almost continuous basis. For the last six months it was assigned to SAC, the in-commission rate varied between a low of 33.2 percent and a high of 74.6 percent while the SAC goal was 80 percent.

On 16 April 1950, the 1st Fighter Wing was redesignated the 1st Fighter-Interceptor Wing, a more appropriate designator. The wing was relieved from assignment to SAC and assigned to the Continental Air Command for air defense purposes on 1 July 1950, thereby ending the 14-month service of the F-86 in SAC.

F-84, Thunderjet, Thunderstreak, and Thunderflash. Any history of fighters in the Strategic Air Command would have to emphasize the F-84. Several models were assigned and in greater numbers than any other fighter. In fact, more F-84s were assigned than all other fighters combined. Furthermore, they were assigned for the longest period of time--from June to December 1948 and from September 1949 to 1 July 1957. In addition, the F-84 had become the standard jet fighter for SAC's fighter force and contributed to the stability in the fighter program that was characteristic after 1950. There is no doubt it was the workhorse. The first were the F-84Bs.

Pilots of the 33rd Fighter Wing flew the first F-84Bs assigned to SAC to Roswell AFB (later renamed Walker), New Mexico, from the Republic Aviation Corporation factory in Long Island, New York. The first five arrived on 9 June 1948 and by the end of the month 47 F-84Bs were in place. The peak strength of F-84Bs in the 33rd Fighter Wing

---

* On 1 July 1957, the 65th Air Division (Defense) located in Spain was assigned to SAC and the 16th Air Force (SAC GO 35, 4 Jun 57). On 5 July 1958, the 497th Fighter-Interceptor Squadron was relieved from assignment to ADC and assigned to SAC and the 65th Air Division (SAC GO 37, 14 Jul 58). On 1 September 1958, the 431st Fighter-Interceptor Squadron was also relieved from assignment to ADC and assigned to SAC and the 65th Air Division (SAC GO 52, 15 Aug 58). These two F-86 squadrons were under the operational control of USAFE for air base air defense, but assigned to SAC air base groups at Torrejon and Zaragoza for administration and logistics support. On 1 July 1960, they were relieved from assignment to the 16th Air Force and assigned to USAFE (SAC GO 43, 1 May 60).

F-86A Sabrejet assigned to SAC's 1st Fighter Wing at March AFB, California in 1950.

rose to 83 aircraft during the month of October 1948. They did not
remain long. On 16 November 1948, the 33rd Fighter Wing began a move
from Roswell AFB to Otis AFB, Massachusetts, and on 1 December 1948 the
wing was relieved from assignment to SAC and assigned to the Continental
Air Command for air defense purposes.

First experiences with the F-84B were unfavorable. Maintenance
problems were enormous. During July 1948, 54 percent of the aircraft on
hand were out of commission because of maintenance and eight percent
because of parts. This drastic situation of only 38 percent of the
wing's aircraft being operationally ready improved gradually in the
period until the F-84s were transferred out of SAC on 1 December 1948.
The major cause of the maintenance problem was the short life before
failure. Furthermore, F-84 engine changes expended five times the
number of manhours required for an engine change on an F-80.

After the 1 December 1948 reassignment of the 33rd Fighter
Wing, it was nearly a year before the F-84s were again assigned to SAC.
In September 1949, the first F-84s began arriving at Bergstrom AFB,
Texas, for the 27th Fighter-Escort Wing. The F-84E was an improved
version of the F-84B with a better engine, better control systems, and
with better crew comfort by means of a larger cockpit. In addition, it
was the first fighter equipped with a radar gun sight and it had
improved wing-tip tanks. From the September 1949 assignments until
the fighters were terminated in SAC on 1 July 1957, F-84s in several
models constituted the main body of fighter escorts. By early 1950, the
F-84Es were readily available from the production lines. Each suc-
ceeding model was an attempt to alleviate the basic design deficiencies
in the F-84: insufficient range and inadequate speed for the escort
mission.

The 27th Fighter Escort Wing was the first unit to convert to
the F-84E and the difficulties it encountered during the conversion
caused the wing to retain its F-82E Twin Mustang aircraft until the end
of August 1950. In spite of the problems this created for the supply
and maintenance functions with two sets of parts, etc., retention of the
conventional F-82E was considered necessary because the new aircraft
were not considered mechanically sound prior to delivery. Subsequent
modifications caused the 27th Fighter Escort Wing to be more of a test
unit than allowing the unit to train with the new aircraft. Regardless, the training progressed at such a rapid rate that the crews of the
27th were able to pick up 262 F-84E aircraft at the factory between
March and September 1950, flying them to Bergstrom AFB on shakedown sorties, and then ferry 180 of them overseas in September and October 1950.
In addition, the 27th was ordered in November to depart for the Far East
and combat operations with the F-84Es. All these efforts were
accomplished during a period that could only be classed as hectic.
There were many problems, including delay in initial deliveries. For
example, the ferrying of 180 F-84Es overseas in September and October
1950 had originally been scheduled for May 1950. By 30 June 1950, only

74

52 aircraft had been delivered from the factory. In addition, continued engine failures reached such proportions in May and June 1950 that the aircraft were grounded. Solutions were found, but the deployment had been postponed four months.

The other two wings equipped with the F-84E were the 12th and 31st Fighter-Escort Wings. The 31st was equipped with F-84Es when it was assigned on 1 July 1950. On 5 December 1950, the 12th Fighter-Escort Wing moved to Bergstrom from Turner. Its first F-84E aircraft arrived at Bergstrom on 13 December and its assets at the end of the year were nine F-84Es. It built up to UE strength of 75 in early 1951 and deployed to the United Kingdom on rotation in July 1951. The 12th deployed without its aircraft and assumed accountability for the F-84Es from the 31st which then returned to the United States. When the 12th Fighter-Escort Wing returned from overseas in December 1951, the F-84Es were left in England for the 123rd Fighter-Bomber Wing and the 12th was reequipped with F-84Gs upon its return.

When the Korean War made more USAF funds available, the SAC fighter program was one of the recipients. The ultimate objective of the fighter program was to equip all SAC fighter wings with the F-84F, but they would not be available until late 1953. In the meantime, SAC would receive F-84Gs. Since the first F-84E had been assigned to SAC in September 1949, its service with the command only encompassed two years until the conversion program to replace it with the F-84Gs began in September 1951. There were few training problems associated with the conversion since the characteristics of the two aircraft were similar. The differences between the two aircraft's capabilities were significant. Two features were outstanding. The F-84G was the first single-seat fighter aircraft that could deliver an atomic bomb. It had provisions for being refueled from a boom-equipped tanker. In addition, the F-84G was equipped with an autopilot necessary for the longer missions. It was powered by an improved engine and was able to carry a heavier bomb load. The F-84G was considered an interim aircraft to fill SAC's needs until the more advanced swept-wing F-84F would arrive from the production lines.

The first F-84G models assigned to SAC went to the 27th Fighter- Escort Wing in September 1951, followed in October by others assigned to the 31st Fighter-Escort Wing. The F-84G remained the basic fighter of SAC until mid-1954 when the F-84F began to arrive. Despite the experience SAC had acquired with the F-84E, some of the problems encountered with the F-84Gs were identical. In the first place, the actual number of aircraft delivered to the command fell behind the USAF allocations schedules. As of 1 February 1952, the allocation was such that the three fighter wings of SAC were supposed to be fully equipped with 225 UE aircraft. The actual number possessed did not reach 225 until July 1952. The slippage followed the pattern established by the other models and the development of combat readiness in the wings was delayed accordingly. The slippage in the delivery of F-84Gs to SAC remained constant. It was compounded by the activation of a fourth fighter wing, the 508th at Turner AFB, on 1 July 1952. Headquarters SAC decided that the tactical sections of the 508th would be manned at only two-thirds of authorization because of the aircraft shortages. Aircraft equipping of the wing began in July but with only 30 aircraft, and these were assigned by taking 15 each from the 27th and 31st wings. No levies were taken from the 12th wing because of its commitments to Project Ivy (see section "Long-Range and Overseas Deployments"). Thus, the F-84G assets of the four fighter wings were as follows:

Unit	F-84Gs Authorized
12th	75
27th	60
31st	60
508th	30

The aircraft shortage in the assets of F-84Gs began to ease in September 1952 with the increase in allocations and improved in 1953 with additional production. These changes permitted a more rapid buildup of the 508th wing than was expected previously. However, these shortages were quickly aggravated by the activation of two additional strategic fighter wings in 1953 (see Appendix II, SAC Fighter Units). On 24 January 1953, the 506th Strategic Fighter Wing was activated at Dow AFB and it began receiving its fighters in April. The authorization for fighter aircraft increased accordingly to 375 and in June 1953, SAC had 302 assigned (included are the aircraft TDY to FEAF). On 18 December 1953, the 407th was activated at Great Falls AFB, Montana, and it began receiving its fighter aircraft in March 1954.

F-84Gs were improvements over the F-84Es, but the "G" still failed to satisfy SAC's requirement for support of strategic forces. Major deficiencies were identical with the E: insufficient range and airspeed. The air refueling capacities of the F-84G resolved some of the questions of range, but the F-84G was still considered inadequate.

SAC had begun mid-air refueling for its bomber aircraft in 1948 and the range extension obtained from this practice was applied to the fighters with the F-84G. Once SAC was equipped with the "G", refueling began. In 1951 the tanker aircraft were provided from the squadrons that had the primary mission to support bomber wings. By the fall of 1953, specific air refueling squadrons were activated and assigned to the fighter wings (see Appendix II, SAC Fighter Units). Four of the squadrons were equipped with the KB-20P tanker aircraft and one was equipped with KC-97E tankers. The four KB-29P squadrons were: 27th, 407th, 506th, and 508th Air Refueling Squadrons, Strategic Fighter, and the KC-97E squadron was the 71st. When the fighters left SAC on 1 July 1957, three of the KB-29P squadrons were inactivated. On

76

1 November 1957, the 27th was inactivated as the last KB-29 squadron in
SAC. On 15 December 1957, the 71st Air Refueling Squadron, Strategic
Fighter, was redesignated Air Refueling Squadron, Medium. With air
refueling, SAC fighter wings possessed the ability to deploy nonstop to
overseas locations in Europe, Africa, and the Orient.

The F-84G was not considered adequate for the fighter mission.
Yet for two years, it was the mainstay of the SAC fighter force.
Actually, production of the F-84G could be considered as an interim
fighter program caused as a result of an accident. Republic Aviation
Corporation had started production of fuselages to the successor of the
F-84E as the swept-wing F-84F. A considerable number of F-84F fuselages
had been built based on the accessibility of a newly-developed powerful
engine of English design. During fabrication of the fuselages, negotiations were being conducted to obtain manufacturing rights for the
United States production of this engine. Agreements could not be
reached and the negotiations terminated. When they broke down, Republic
Aviation Corporation had to resume production of the straight-wing 1951
model, the F-84E, for the Air Force, but it was redesignated the F-84G
because of the improvements installed. Jet engines for this aircraft
were readily available. During production of the "Gs", United States
manufacturers developed a jet engine that was suitable for use in the
partially constructed F-84Fs. The new engine was designated J-65 and
installed in the F-84F fuselages that had been shunted aside on the production line.

Delivery slippages for the F-84Gs were mild compared to those
for the F-84Fs. The first delivery scheduled for SAC was to be in
October 1952. The first aircraft were scheduled for the 31st
Fighter-Escort Wing and followed by deliveries to the 27th wing. This
schedule was established in April 1952, and one month later the delivery
date of the first F-84F had already slipped from October 1952 to the
April-June 1953 period with the projections emphasizing April. Then
in March 1953 the delivery date of the first fighter dropped back to
August 1953. The reason justifying these delays was additional engine
testing and subsequent performance improvements. Slippages continued
through the rest of 1953 and the first F-84Fs were assigned to the 506th
Strategic Fighter Wing in January 1954, but even these were inadequately
equipped. The cause for the inadequacies was the engine.

Engine problems haunted the F-84F more than any other F-84.
The first aircraft that were delivered to the 506th wing were equipped
with the YJ-65 engine, a substitute because the J-65 engine constantly
showed deficiencies: aluminum blade failures, fuel control difficulties,
and a high rejection rate of combustion chamber inlet housings and
castings. Because of these serious deficiencies, Headquarters USAF
increased the number of F-84Fs equipped with the substitute YJ-65 engines from the 89 allocated to the 506th to 172 which allowed SAC to equip
the 27th Strategic Fighter Wing. These allocations presented a
disturbing feature. Because of the engine, the aircraft were rated at

"zero" operational readiness. The cause for the rating was that there was no overseas logistical support for the engine, nor was there any intention to establish one.

Once the development and production of the J-65 engines reached a point where they were acceptable to USAF, the flow of F-84F aircraft proceeded rapidly. The first one of the F-84Fs was assigned to the 27th Strategic Fighter Wing on 18 June 1954, and by the end of the year four wings were fully equipped with this particular version. The 508th was in the process of conversion and the 407th wing was scheduled to complete conversion shortly after the first of the year in 1955. As a result of the SAC conversion program, the last F-84G was transferred out of the command in August 1955.

The assignment of F-84Fs with substitute engines and later with J-65 engines that were beset with technical problems, led to adjustments in SAC's programming for the fighter force. Prior to the arrival of F-84Fs with J-65 engines, SAC had planned to divide its six fighter wings into two groups, one group equipped with F-84Fs with YJ-65 engines and the other group equipped with F-84Gs. Of course, this imposed a greatly increased supply and logistics load necessary to support two distinctly different types of aircraft. All of the major components of these two airplanes were different. Nevertheless, SAC's fighter units lived with these conditions during the period of transition.

Five of the strategic fighter wings received F-84Fs in 1954 and the sixth, the 407th, began equipping in January 1955. At the end of 1954, none were rated as combat ready, but by the end of June 1955, all but the 407th had attained that status. One year later, the 508th had been inactivated, but the remaining F-84F units were rated as combat ready.

In the meantime, fighter shortage in the F-84F units was expected to continue until the J-65 engine was cleared of deficiencies. Once this occurred, aircraft with YJ-65 engines would be transferred to other commands. By the end of 1954, all YJ-65 equipped F-84Fs had been transferred. However, there were still serious deficiencies associated with the F-84F that would limit the fighter force unless corrected. They were specifically engine problems, a lack of air refuelable external tanks, very high AOCP rates, and a shortage of certain items of support equipment. By January 1955, several accidents had been attributed to engine deficiencies. Between July and December 1954, the AOCP (aircraft out of commission for parts) rates for the J-65 engines was 20.77 percent. Furthermore, compressor failures caused all J-65 engines with less than 25 hours flight time to be grounded. To eliminate these problems, USAF scheduled a modification program to be conducted simultaneously with the Inspection and Repair as Necessary (IRAN) program starting in May 1955 and to extend through 12 months. There would be 46 F-84Fs in the program at all times.

Materiel shortages and deficiencies continued to hamper the F-84F fleet into early 1955. Procurement programs were in effect by June to eliminate the shortages. Deficiencies, particularly for the engine compressors, were subjects for corrective action.

Both the F-84G and the F-84F fighters were considered inadequate although the latter model provided greater potential. As early as September 1952, Headquarters SAC had concluded that the inherent deficiencies of range and airspeed for both models kept them from being adequate for the SAC mission, especially for the penetration mission. In spite of the long service, these aircraft were actually interim aircraft because long-range planning called for the SAC escort fighter to be the McDonnell F-101A.

F-101A, Voodoo. SAC's possession of a century-series fighter was extremely short in as much as the first few F-101As arrived at a SAC base about the time SAC was relinquishing its fighter force to TAC. Experience with the deliveries of F-84G and F-84F aircraft had been a series of repeated slippages. There was little difference with the F-101A. Initial plans scheduled the first F-101A to SAC's 27th Strategic Fighter Wing in October 1956. In preparation for this delivery date, the 27th Wing was reorganized on F-101A Tables of Organization on 15 July 1956. After several delays, the first F-101A arrived at Bergstrom in May 1957, only to be sent to Air Training Command on a temporary basis. The first three F-101As arrived at Bergstrom on 3 June 1957. Major causes for the delays were deficiencies uncovered during tests conducted at Edwards AFB, California. Headquarters Second Air Force asked Headquarters SAC not to accept the aircraft until the deficiencies had been eliminated and the ability of the F-101A to perform the mission had been firmly established. On 1 July 1957, SAC's fighter units were inactivated or reassigned to TAC. The irony in this was that SAC had struggled with inadequate aircraft for its fighter mission from the beginning. The F-101A was the first aircraft with full potential to execute the mission required. SAC had fought for this aircraft since early 1950, had contributed to the 1952 decision to develop and produce it, had begun the conversion program, and the wing was reassigned to TAC 27 days after the arrival of the first fighters.

Reconnaissance Fighters

From 24 January 1955 to 1 July 1957, SAC possessed one strategic reconnaissance wing, fighter, the 71st, stationed at Larson AFB, Washington. It was an unusual organization in that two of the three tactical squadrons, the 25th and 82nd, were equipped with RF-84F aircraft. The third squadron, the 91st, was equipped with RF-84K aircraft (see Fighter Conveyor (FICON) Program, next page). Delivery of tactical aircraft was a familiar story with a number of delays. On 31 January 1956, a full year after activation, only 19 RF-84F aircraft were possessed. By April this had increased to 45 of the 50 authorized for

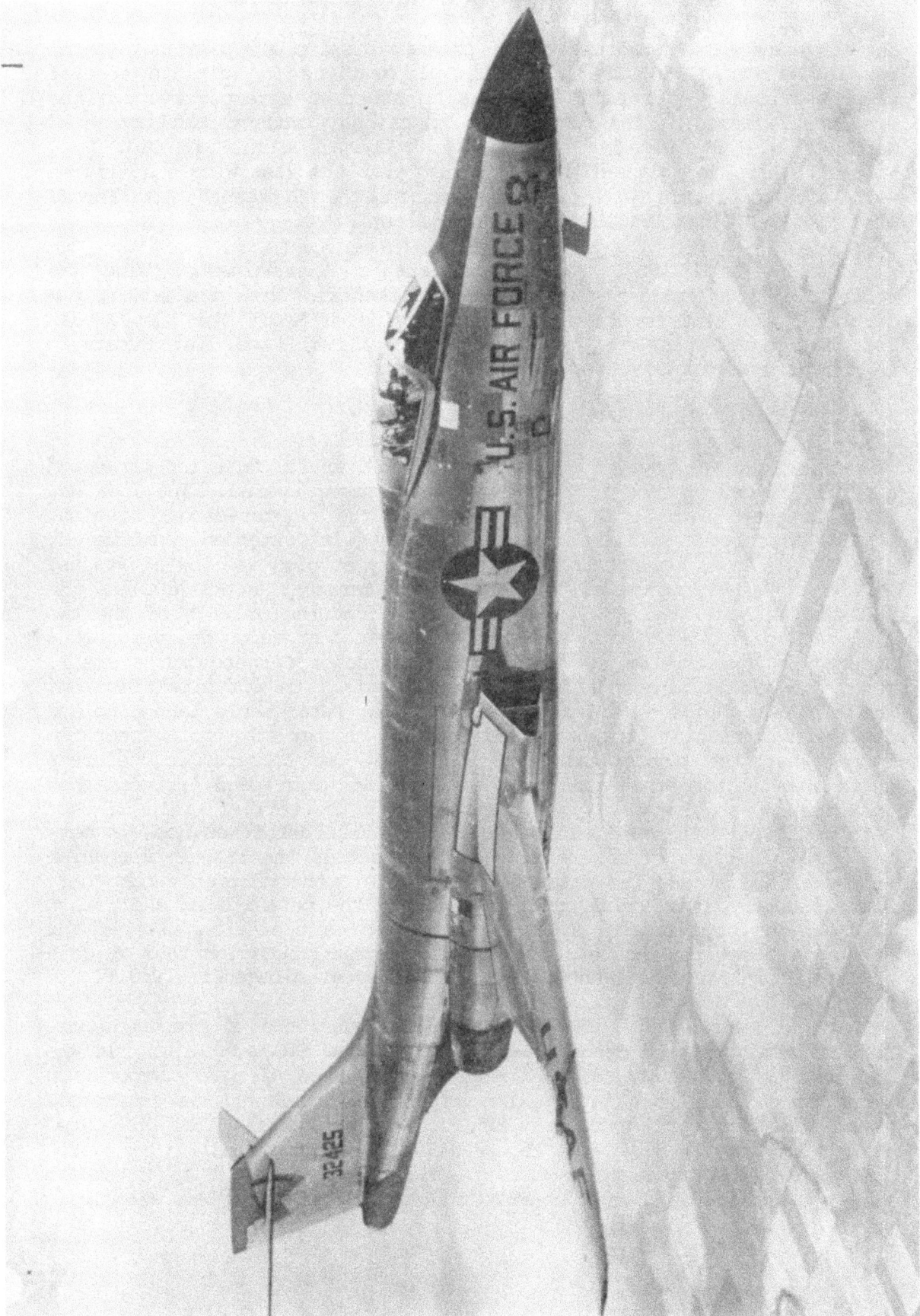

F-101 Voodoo assigned to the 27th Strategic Fighter Wing, Bergstrom AFB, Texas in July 1956.

80

the 25th and 82nd squadrons. The primary mission was reconnaissance, but in February 1956, the wing made preparations to initiate special weapons training at Larson. It was an abortive attempt, because the wing was relieved of the requirement to maintain such capability on 17 March 1956. By December 1956, Major General Archie J. Old, Jr., Fifteenth Air Force Commander, determined that the 71st Wing's abilities were not compatible with the mission of the Fifteenth Air Force. Shortly after, inactivation of the wing began.

On 29 April 1957, the 71st Strategic Reconnaissance Wing was relieved of its emergency war plan commitments. Within a month, the aircraft were sent to training units outside of SAC. The last RF-84K left Larson AFB, in May. Effective 1 July 1957, the 71st Strategic Reconnaissance Wing, Fighter, was inactivated.

Fighter Conveyor (FICON) Program

The Fighter-Conveyor (FICON) Program was a "carrier-parasite" aircraft reconnaissance and strategic bombardment system. The idea was first broached in 1946 in conjunction with the fighter-escort mission. The FICON program was designed to provide SAC with extended, unrefueled, high-speed reconnaissance and atomic delivery at high and low altitudes. The means was through an airborne aircraft carrier, an RB-36D, and the parasite fighter, the RF-84K. The design features of each of the two components contributed to a system that provided a weapon delivery technique that was capable of reaching a long-range target with a small, fast, and highly maneuverable fighter aircraft. On a typical mission, the long-range bomber, equipped with a rigid, retractable launching and retrieving mechanism (trapeze), carried the fighter to a point near the target where the fighter was dropped. The RD-36D loitered in the areas while the fighter penetrated to the target at high speed, accomplished its mission, and returned to rendezvous with the carrier. The RF-84Ds were modified with a retractable mechanism that permitted hookups between the two types of aircraft. Once connected, the trapeze mechanism supported and stowed the parasite fighter into the carrier's bomb bay. After recovery, the bomber then transported the parasite on the return trip to the home base. This carrier-parasite operation allowed the strategic forces to choose the exact geographical location from which a combat sortie could be launched. The FICON Program began in 1950.

On 23 March 1950, Headquarters SAC submitted a proposed concept of operations to Headquarters USAF for the FICON Program. It was approved and in January 1951, Consolidated Vultee Aircraft Corporation began work. One year later, the first contact flight was attempted. Because of the early successes of FICON, Headquarters USAF allocated funds for ten RB-36Ds and 25 RF-84Fs to be modified. The 348th Strategic Reconnaissance Squadron, Heavy, of the 99th Strategic Reconnaissance Wing, Heavy, at Fairchild AFB, Washington, was selected to have its aircraft modified for the carrier configuration. The 25 RF-84Fs were to be assigned to the 91st Strategic Reconnaissance Squadron, Fighter, which had been redesignated from the 91st Strategic Reconnaissance Squadron, Medium (Photographic), assigned to SAC from FEAF, and attached to the 407th Strategic Fighter Wing at Malmstrom AFB, Montana, effective 20 December 1953. On 24 January 1955, the 91st Strategic Reconnaissance Squadron, Fighter, was assigned to the 71st Strategic Reconnaissance Wing, Fighter. On 17 July 1955, the squadron moved from Malmstrom to Larson AFB.

RB-36D Modification

1954				1955												Total
S	O	N	D	J	F	M	A	M	J	J	A	S	O	N	D	
1	1	2	3	3												10

RF-84F/K

S	O	N	D	J	F	M	A	M	J	J	A	S	O	N	D	Total
	1	1	2	2	3	3	3	3	3	2	1	1				25

There was a slippage in the program. Production delays postponed the initial delivery of the RF-84F/K aircraft. The initial scheduled delivery had been for November 1954 and the date was first moved back to reestablish the arrival date for April 1955. Actually, the first RF-84K did not arrive until 16 July 1955. The slippage in the conversion program for the RB-36D was even more drastic. The schedule had placed the first aircraft with SAC in September 1954. It did not arrive until 26 November 1955. Only 23 RF-84Ks and seven RB-36Ds were produced.

Shortly after the first arrival, the first hookup of the FICON system flown by SAC crews and away from the Consolidated Vultee Aircraft Corporation plant at Fort Worth, Texas, took place in early December 1955 in the immediate vicinity of Larson AFB. By January 1956, FICON operations were being flown on a regular basis by the two FICON squadrons. Although there were many successes, there were several incidents occurring during the hookups. For example, three fighter aircraft of six attempting hookups were damaged on the first day of training. In February 1956, Headquarters SAC requested that the program be terminated. Headquarters USAF agreed.

APPENDIX II

SAC FIGHTER UNITS AND NUMBERED AIR FORCES

UNIT	BASE	DATES	NUMBERED AIR FORCE
1st	March	1 May 49–1 Jul 50	15th
4th	Selfridge	9 Sep 46–1 Apr 47	15th
	Andrews	1 Apr 47–1 Dec 48	HQ SAC
12th	Turner	1 Nov 50–5 Dec 50	2nd
	Bergstrom	5 Dec 50–1 Apr 55	8th
	Bergstrom	1 Apr 55–1 Jul 57	2nd
27th	Andrews	25 Jun 47–16 Jul 47	HQ SAC
	Kearney	16 Jul 47–16 Mar 49	8th
	Bergstrom	16 Mar 49–1 Apr 55	8th
	Bergstrom	1 Apr 55–1 Jul 57	2nd
31st	Turner	1 Jul 50–1 Apr 57	2nd
33rd	Walker	16 Sep 47–16 Nov 48	8th
	Otis	16 Nov 48–1 Dec 48	8th
56th	Selfridge	1 May 46–1 Oct 47	15th
	Selfridge	1 Oct 47–1 Dec 48	HQ SAC
71st	Larson	24 Jan 55–1 Jul 57	15th
82nd	Bolling	27 Jun 46–21 Oct 46	HQ SAC
	Andrews	21 Oct 46–12 Apr 47	HQ SAC
	Grenier	12 Apr 47–16 Dec 48	HQ SAC
	Grenier	16 Dec 48–22 Aug 49	15th
87th (USAFR)	Bergstrom	27 Jun 49–25 Jun 51	8th
108th(ANG)	Turner	16 Mar 51–15 Nov 51	2nd
131st(ANG)	Bergstrom	10 Mar 51–4 Aug 51	8th
	George	4 Aug 51–16 Nov 51	15th
132nd(ANG)	Dow	16 Apr 51–16 Nov 51	8th
146th(ANG)	Moody	17 Apr 51–16 Nov 51	2nd

APPENDIX II (Cont)

SAC FIGHTER UNITS AND NUMBERED AIR FORCES

UNIT	BASE	DATES	NUMBERED AIR FORCE
506th	Dow	20 Jan 53-3 Feb 55	8th
	Tinker	3 Feb 55-1 Apr 55	8th
	Tinker	1 Apr 55-1 Jul 57	2nd
508th	Turner	1 Jul 52-11 May 56	2nd

APPENDIX III

CHARACTERISTICS OF SAC FIGHTER AIRCRAFT

P-47D/N

Manufacturer: Republic Aviation Corporation, Long Island, New York and Evansville, Indiana. Curtiss-Wright Corporation, Buffalo, New York

Type: Single seat escort fighter

Crew: Pilot in enclosed cockpit

	P-47D	P-47N
Power Plant:	2,300 hp R-2800-59	2,800 hp R-2800-77
Dimensions:		
Span	40 feet 9 inches	42 feet 7 inches
Length	36 feet 1 inch	36 feet 1 inch
Height	14 feet 2 inches	14 feet 8 inches
Wing Area	300 square feet	322 square feet
Weights:		
Empty	10,000 pounds	11,000 pounds
Gross	19,400 pounds	20,700 pounds
Performance:		
Maximum speed	428 mph at 30,000 ft	467 mph at 32,500 ft
Cruising speed	350 mph	300 mph
Climb	9 minutes to 20,000 ft	14 minutes 12 seconds to 25,000 ft
Service Ceiling	42,000 feet	43,000 feet
Range, ferry	475 statute miles	800 statute miles

Armament: Eight .50 caliber machine guns and two 1,000-pound bombs, external

SOURCE: Swanborough, Gordon and Bowers, P. M., United States Military Aircraft Since 1908, Putnam, London, 1963, pp 460-461.

P-51H

Manufacturer: North American Aviation, Inc., Inglewood, California, and Dallas, Texas

Type: Single-seat fighter, ground attack, and long-range escort

Crew: Pilot in enclosed cockpit

Power Plant: 1,380 hp
                       V-1650-9

Dimensions:
Span	37 feet
Length	33 feet, 4 inches
Height	13 feet, 8 inches
Wing Area	233 square feet

Weights:
Empty	6,585 pounds
Gross	11,054 pounds

Performance:
Maximum speed	487 mph at 25,000 feet
Cruising speed	380 mph
Climb	12.5 minutes to 30,000 feet
Service ceiling	41,600 feet
Range, ferry	850 statute miles

Armament: Six .50 caliber machine guns or
                              Ten 5-inch rockets

SOURCE: Swanborough, Gordon and Bowers, P. M., United States Military Aircraft Since 1908, Putnam, London, 1963, pp 408-414.

P-82E

Manufacturer: North American Aviation, Inc., Inglewood, California

Type: Long-range escort fighter

Crew: Two pilots in individual enclosed cockpits

Power Plant: Two 1,600 hp; Allison V-1710-143/145 piston Vee in-line

Dimensions:
Span	51 feet 3 inches
Length	42 feet 5 inches
Height	13 feet 10 inches
Wing Area	408 square feet

Weights:
Empty	15,997 pounds
Gross	25,591 pounds

Performance:
Maximum speed	461 mph at 21,000 feet
Crusiing speed	286 mph
Climb, initial	3,770 feet per minute
Service ceiling	38,900 feet
Range, ferry	2,240 statute miles

Armament: Six .50 caliber machine guns in wing center section
Four 1,000-pound bombs external

SOURCE: Swanborough, Gordon and Bowers, P. M., United States Military Aircraft Since 1908, Putnam, London, 1963, pp 415-416.

P-80A

Manufacturer: Lockheed Aircraft Corporation, Burbank, California

Type: Fighter

Crew: Pilot in enclosed cockpit

Power Plant: 4,000-pound st; J-33-A-11

Dimensions:

Span	39 feet 11 inches
Length	34 feet 6 inches
Height	11 feet 4 inches
Wing Area	238 square feet

Weights:

Empty	7,920 pounds
Gross	14,500 pounds

Performance:

Maximum speed	558 mph at 7,000 feet
Cruising speed	410 mph
Climb	4,500 feet per minute
Service ceiling	45,000 feet
Range, ferry	540 miles

Armament	Six .50 caliber machine guns

SOURCE: Swanborough, Gordon and Bowers, P. M., United States Military Aircraft Since 1908, Putnam, London, 1963, pp 334-339.

F-86A

Manufacturer: North American Aviation, Inc., Inglewood, California

Type: Fighter and Fighter-Bomber

Crew: Pilot in enclosed cockpit

Power Plant:	5,200 pound s.t. J-47-GE-13
Dimensions:	
Span	37 feet 1 inch
Length	37 feet 6 inches
Height	14 feet 8 inches
Wing Area	288 square feet
Weights:	
Empty	10,495 pounds
Gross	16,357 pounds
Performance:	
Maximum speed	672 mph at 2,500 feet
Cruising speed	527 mph
Climb, initial	7,630 feet per minute
Service ceiling	48,300 feet
Range, ferry	785 miles
Armament:	Six .50 caliber machine guns, Two 1,000-pound bombs or 16 5-inch rockets.

SOURCE: Swanborough, Gordon and Bowers, P. M., United States Military
Aircraft Since 1908, Putnam, London, 1963, pp 422-426.

F-101A

Manufacturer: McDonnell Aircraft Corporation, St. Louis, Missouri

Type: Interceptor Fighter and Tactical Fighter-Bomber

Crew: Pilot in enclosed cockpit

Power Plant: Two 10,100-pound (14,880-pound with afberburner) Pratt
and Whitner J57-P-13 turbojet engines

Dimensions:
Span	39 feet 8 inches
Length	67 feet 4-3/4 inches
Height	18 feet
Wing Area	368 square feet

Weight:
Gross	46,500 pounds

Performance:
Maximum speed	1,220 mph at 40,000 feet
Cruising speed	595 mph at 36,000 feet
Climb, initial	14,000 feet per minute
Service ceiling	51,000 feet
Range, ferry	2,200 statute miles

Armament: Three AIM-4D Falcon air-to-air missiles in internal bomb bay, and two AIR-2A Genie missiles under fuselage.

SOURCE: 1. Swanborough, Gordon and Bowers, P. M., United States
Military Aircraft Since 1908, Putnam, London, 1963, pp 363-365
2. Rpt (S/RD), AFSC(RTD), Air Force Guide No 1, "USAF Aircraft
Characteristics Summary (U) (Black Book)," F-101A.

F-84E/G/F

Manufacturer: Republic Aviation Corporation, Long Island, New York and
General Motors Corporation, Kansas City, Missouri

Type: Fighter, Fighter-bomber, Fighter-escort

Crew: Pilot in enclosed cockpit

Power Plant:	F-84E	F-84G	F-84F
	5,600 pound s.t.	5,600 pound s.t. J-35-A-29	7,800 pound s.t. J65-W-3 J65-W-7 in RF

Dimensions:

	F-84E	F-84G	F-84F
Span	36 feet 5 inches	36 feet 5 inches	33 feet 7$\frac{1}{4}$ inches
Length	37 feet 5 inches	38 feet 1 inch	43 feet 4-3/4 in
Height	12 feet 10 inches	12 feet 7 inches	14 feet 4-3/4 in (15 feet RF)
Wing Area	260 square feet	260 square feet	_____

Weights:

	F-84E	F-84G	F-84F
Empty	9,538 pounds	11,095 pounds	_____
Gross	19,689 pounds	23,525 pounds	28,000 pounds

Performance:

	F-84E	F-84G	F-84F
Maximum speed	587 @ 4,000	622 @ 0	695 @ 0
Cruising spped	436 mph	483 mph	
Climb	4,210 ft/min	9.4 min to 35,000 ft	8,200 ft/min (8,000 ft/min RF)
Service ceiling	40,750 feet	40,000 feet	46,000 feet
Range, ferry	1,282 statue miles	2,000 statute miles	2,200 statute miles

Armament:

F-84E	F-84G	F-84F
Four .50 caliber machine guns 32 5-in rockets	Six .50 caliber machine guns (4 in RF) 32 5-in rockets, Two 1,000 pound bombs	6,000 pounds in bombs

SOURCE: Swanborough, Gordon and Bowers, P. M., United States Military Aircraft Since 1908, Putnam, London, 1963, pp 462-468.

APPENDIX IV

SAC FIGHTER AIRCRAFT INVENTORY (Assigned)

As of	P/F-47	P/F-51	P/F-80	P/F-82	F-84	F-86	F-101
31 Dec 46	17	85	2				
30 Jun 47	11	42	126				
31 Dec 47	3	230	120	1			
30 Jun 48		229	112	31	47*		
31 Dec 48		131	1	81	7		
30 Jun 49		97		81		82	
31 Dec 49				75	3	77	
30 Jun 50				59	52	80	
31 Dec 50					75		
30 Jun 51	80	107			170		
31 Dec 51					75		
30 Jun 52					212		
31 Dec 52					230		
30 Jun 53					235		
31 Dec 53					235		
30 Jun 54					314		
31 Dec 54					411		
30 Jun 55					511		
31 Dec 55					568**		
30 Jun 56					506**		
31 Dec 56					389**		
30 Jun 57					181		

---

*   (U) Hist 8AF, Jan–Jun 48, p 86.
** (U) Included RF-84F/K.
SOURCE: Rpt (U), SAC Comptroller, "Summary of SAC Operational Data (U),"
         as of dates indicated.

APPENDIX V

UNIT ASSIGNMENTS

UNIT	AIRCRAFT TYPE	FIRST AIRCRAFT RECEIVED
1st	F-86A	1 May 49
4th	(P-51H)	9 Sep 46
	P-80A	23 Apr 47
12th	F-84E	13 Dec 50
	F-84G	Dec 51
	F-84F	Jan 54
27th	(P-51H)	25 Jun 47
	P-82E	23 Jan 48
	F-84E	Sep 49
	F-84G	Sep 51
	F-84F	18 Jun 54
	F-101A	3 May 57
31st	F-84E	1 Jul 50
	F-84G	Oct 51
	F-84F	21 Oct 54
33rd	P-51H	Oct 47
	F-84B	9 Jun 48
56th	P-51H	Jun 46
	P-80A	23 Apr 47
71st	RF-84F/K	Mar 55
82nd	(P-82E)	27 Jun 46
	P-51H	15 Aug 47
108th(ANG)	F-47D	16 Mar 51
131st(ANG)	F-51D	16 Apr 51
	F-84B/C	16 Apr 51
146th(ANG)	F-51D	17 Apr 51
407th	F-84G	Mar 54
	F-84F	1 Nov 54
506th	F-84G	Apr 53
	F-84F	Mar 54
508th	F-84G	1 Jul 52
	F-84F	28 Nov 54

☆U.S. GOVERNMENT PRINTING OFFICE: 1988-554-000/81021